The Sounds of Feminist Theory

SUNY series in Feminist Criticism and Theory
Michelle A. Massé, Editor

The Sounds of Feminist Theory

RUTH SALVAGGIO

For Glo —
I hope you find
some of The sounds of This
Theory echoing in your
own music and
writing —

January 23, 1999

State University of New York Press

Published by
State University of New York Press, Albany

For information, address State University of New York Press,
State University Plaza, Albany, NY 12246

Production by M. R. Mulholland
Marketing by Fran Keneston

Library of Congress Cataloging-in-Publication Data

Salvaggio, Ruth.
    The sounds of feminist theory / Ruth Salvaggio.
        p.   cm. — (SUNY series in feminist criticism and theory)
    Includes bibliographical references and index.
    ISBN 0-7914-4013-3 (alk. paper). — ISBN 0-7914-4014-1 (pbk. :
alk. paper)
        1. Feminist literary criticism.   2. Women and literature.
    3. Feminism and literature.   I. Title.   II. Series.
PN98.W64S25   1999
801'.95'082—dc21   98-6221
                                                                            CIP

10 9 8 7 6 5 4 3 2 1

CONTENTS

Acknowledgments

I'm most grateful to Minrose Gwin, who read more versions of this manuscript than she would admit, for support over the long haul and for continual discerning readings of my work; and to my mother, Zenobia Riley Salvaggio, whose love for language caught fire in me, and whose influence on this book is more than she would imagine.

Thanks to my colleagues at the University of New Mexico, Michael Fischer, Vera Norwood, Shane Phelan, Diana Robin, and Carolyn Woodward, for reading parts of the manuscript, and especially Marta Weigle for our discussions of oral language traditions. Thanks to Margaret Randall particularly for her thoughtful comments on the final chapter; to Janice Gould for exchanges about orality and poetry; and to Grace Bauer and Ellen Brown for early guidance. I learned much from my PhD student, Constance Morris Shortlidge, who died while this book was in press; her work on feminist theory and vision enhanced my own attention to sound.

I am grateful to Katherine Soniat for permission to reprint her poem "Cracking Eggs," from her collection *Cracking Eggs,* Copyright 1990 by the University of Central Florida Press; to Yale University Press for permission to reprint Olga Broumas's poem "Artemis" from her collection *Beginning with O,* Copyright 1977 by Yale University Press; and to Indiana University Press for permission to reprint portions of my essay "Skin Deep: Lesbian Interventions in Language," which appeared in the anthology *Cross Purposes: Lesbians, Feminists, and the Limits of Alliance,* edited by Dana Heller, Copyright 1997 by Indiana University Press, and which is recast here in my chapter "Queer Curves."

I've benefited from the sharp and shaping critique of three readers for SUNY Press, Suzanne Woods and two anonymous readers. It has been a pleasure to work with James Peltz, Editor at SUNY Press, and Michelle Massé, editor of the Feminist Theory and Criticism Series at SUNY, both of whom made the editing process seem easy. I am obviously in debt to the numerous feminist theorists whose writings are the subject of this book; I hope that they might approve at least some of what I have to say.

Finally, I want to thank the anonymous woman in San Sulpice, who conducted the singing during a Catholic mass I unexpectedly attended one fine morning in Paris. I was drawn into this austere doric cathedral on my way to museums; theories of feminine language were the absolute last thing on my mind. The cathedral was scattered with male iconography: statues and stained glass, priests and deacons, and the bright yellow windows in back of the altar where Christ himself was fast ascending into heaven. A slim woman approached the side altar to lead our congregation in singing. She sang in a high clear voice, and had this way of waving one hand—waving it smoothly and rhythmically—to conduct our voices. I can't remember what we sang, but I recall her voice moving like a sound wave through the architecture, as if it were dissolving this grand male enclave and all its visual maintenance. The mass and its messages seemed to melt.

Of course I realize that this was not some revelation, just my own narrative of what happened that morning. But since I have come, over the years, to invest in the power of certain narratives, I couldn't help but read this one as a nostalgia for certain theories of feminine language and all its pre-oedipal rhythms and pulsations, semiotic fusions, its oral tonalities and sheer vocal disruption. And since one's scholarly career, I suppose, involves discarding some theoretical baggage while keeping choice remnants on hand, I can safely say that I have let go of most of these appealing yet potentially deterministic theories about female voice. But I've continued to listen for their sounds.

I heard them that morning in San Sulpice. I think that's when I began to contemplate this book.

PREFACE: HEARING THE O

IS THE MOTION OF WORDS LIKE SOUND?

In her poem "Artemis," Olga Broumas yearns for a moving, rounding language, for words that arch and spiral,

> like a curviform alphabet
> that defies
> decoding, appears
> to consist of vowels, beginning with O, the O-
> mega, horseshoe, the cave of sound. (23)

In her critical essay "The Evidence of Experience," historian Joan Scott suggests that as critics we might glean crucial messages by "reading for 'the literary,'" following the ways in which language moves as it evokes complex and contested interpretations (386). Questioning simplistic links between vision and knowledge, she turns away from the idea that writing is a mere "transmission" of truth, and urges us to notice how the medium of language is continually altering what we see, and therefore what we know. Her metaphor for this undertaking comes from Samuel Delany's autobiographical work *The Motion of Light in Water*, where Delany's vision is mediated, as literary critic Karen Swann describes, in "'dim blue light, whose distorting, refracting qualities produce a wavering of the visible . . . an apprehension of the moving, differing properties of the representational medium—the motion of light in water'" (384).

This book is my effort to meld the poet's "cave of sound" with the critic's attention to language as a "wavering of the visible." As Scott explains (and as myriad feminist scholars have echoed in some fashion or other), the "metaphor of visibility" will go only so far in helping us follow the changing and refracting properties of language as a medium. I suggest that Broumas's configuration of the O—her sounding, curviform alphabet—can put us more closely in touch with the possible meanings generated by a mobile language and epistemology. For if, as so many contemporary theorists have reminded us, truth is not fixed but always relational and moving, then the motion of its words, its medium, is like sound. I want to ponder why feminist critics have chosen to follow the curves of this motion.

Taking feminist theory as my subject, I read and listen for the sounds of words, try to develop a sense for what and how they signify, follow their motion and meanings as they resonate in a broad range of contemporary scholarship. I have in mind not simply metaphors for sound and voice, though descriptions of polyvocality, dialogic exchange, cries, murmurs, semiotic eruptions, and buzzing discourse permeate contemporary critical theory. I mean the actual *effects* of sounding, wavering language in critical and theoretical writing—a distinctive turn toward the oral within the panorama of contemporary thought. My project is therefore about the necessary fusion of sound and knowledge, the aural and critical, ear and epistemology. I call this project "Hearing the O."

What I have to say about the emergence of this sounding language unfolds within the linguistic turn that has come to inform so many contemporary ideas about how language both reflects and constructs, represents and continually mediates reality. Cultural theorists in particular have become increasingly aware of the role language plays in critique, what Stuart Hall describes as "the crucial importance of language and of the linguistic metaphor to *any* study of culture; the expansion of the notion of text and textuality, both as a source of meaning, and as that which escapes and postpones meaning; the recognition of the heterogeneity, of the multiplicity, of meanings, of the struggle to close arbitrarily the infinite semiosis beyond meaning . . ." (283). As a result, we have all become remarkably self-conscious, as critical writers, of how our language inevitably means more than it says, and how it may also question ideas that its very terms continue to reinscribe. Even to utter the word "woman" may at once validate a category or critique its reference; limit its signification or propel its possible implications; confirm, reject, reinvent its meaning.

Feminist theorists, especially those with a fine ear for language and discourse that have reinscribed women in myriad and restrictive ways, are especially familiar with this scenario. As Scott puts the matter, "When . . . we take the disciplines as analysts and producers of cultural knowledge, we find that what is at stake is not simply a literary technique for reading but an epistemological theory that offers a method for analyzing the processes by which meanings are made, by which we make meanings" (8–9). How indeed are meanings made and questioned, stipulated, analyzed, denied, negotiated, resisted, re-created in critical writing? Can critical writing, by feminists or anyone, evade a language that is already heavily cloaked with meanings? Judith Butler poses similar questions: "But I am writing here now: is it too late? Can this writing, can any writing, refuse the terms by which it is appropriated even as, to some extent, that very colonizing discourse enables or produces this stumbling block, this resistance? How do I relate the paradoxical situation of this dependency and refusal?" ("Imitation" 14).

Engaging language on which we inevitably depend, yet whose very terms we must often refuse, critics have become notoriously "writerly" creatures, to use Eve Sedgwick's term ("Against Epistemology" 134)—playing with words in the midst of serious intellectual pursuits. The result is that much critical writing *sounds* different. And feminist criticism, I believe, has especially indulged this sounding language in its theoretical articulations. Words suggest all sorts of messages, some embraced, others cast off, still others remaining imprecise, ambiguous. Rachael DuPlessis describes her own engagement with words: "The practice of anguage. The anguish of language. The anger of language" (165).

The word "language" begins to sound like "anguish," and then "anger." Each word moves, through sound, to the next, then curves back, not only suggesting other words and concepts, but implicating us in the tangled, complex maneuvers of signification and meaning.

The varieties of feminist theory I explore here willingly engage these maneuvers. Their writers do not want to let language lie still. There are no permanent referents for words. The world of theory is not specular, holding forth the promise of clear vision and signification. Rather, language suggests, evokes, resonates. Susan Griffin works her way through the alphabet, from "Backwash" through "Blizzard" and "Bute" to "Moraine" and "Nadir" and "Plain," pondering the possibilities of such linguistic transmutations: "We are living in a matrix of our own sounds" (*Woman* 194).

Listening to these sounds has led me through the looking glass, within and beyond vision, and into this book. Mirrors are familiar metaphors for feminists who write about language. I think, at least, of Luce Irigaray's plunge to the "other side" of the looking glass in her critique of specular language and thought; Trinh Minh-ha's "mirror–writing box," which reflects and refracts any potentially complete, finished sentence; Kaja Silverman's *Acoustic Mirror*, through which the female voice emerges in psychoanalysis and cinema. Vision itself has become hotly contested within feminist scholarship, from critiques of a central, phallic gaze in film theory to Donna Haraway's reclamation of "partial vision" as a means of shifting positions and generating affinity. Teresa de Lauretis's description of "strategies of representation," which have the ability to "alter the standard of vision . . . *of what can be seen*" might well describe much of the feminist project of recovering what remains hidden and suppressed in an all-too-visibly gendered world.[1]

Yet even within the varied feminist critiques of a specular economy, I believe we need to fine-tune our own audible senses as we read and write, listening carefully to *what can be heard*. I say this not to turn away from vision and embrace sound as an alternative mode of communication (another false dichotomy), but to begin to discern the effects of sound as they emerge within the visual economy of the written, printed word. Sonorous language is often regarded as a vehicle of rhythmic poetic expression, and associated with the discourses of passion, madness, lyrical outburst, and semiotic effusion.[2] But there is more to sound than purely sonorous excess. I believe we need also to develop an ear for the finer modulations of language, especially the distinctive effects of sound in articulating thought and analysis. Why is it that Sedgwick feels "cheered up" when she realizes that a controversial essay she wrote begins with a rhythmic iambic pentameter sentence? Why does Luce Irigaray, addressing Friedrich Nietzsche, claim that she was his captive "voice," his "resonance"? Why does Patricia Williams invest so much energy in the vocal telling of stories to her classes and her readers? What critical investment does Julia Kristeva make in the sonorous, semiotic disposition of language, or Donna Haraway in the linguistic process of "articulation"?[3]

In pondering these questions, I have found myself tracing myriad ways in which feminist critics have immersed themselves in the rich linguistic resources of sound. In doing this, they have shaped critical theory into a sphere where sound carries thought along very specific conduits, and where the world of speculation resonates through an audible linguistic medium.

As critics, I believe that it is our task to negotiate our ways through these sounding significations. While I continue to be impressed with much of feminist theory's remarkably situated and dialogic powers of articulation, its embodied thought and expression, its rhythmic and narrative pulsations, I do not think we should succumb to an uncritical celebration of so-called feminine modes of language that emphasize the personal, subjective, emotive, and potentially liberatory dimensions of voice. For this reason, I do not rehearse here the all-too-familiar story of women writers coming to voice after long silence. That narrative, which indeed threads its way throughout so much history, needs to be reiterated in all its myriad and often tragic contexts. Yet like many revolutionary claims, it can move all too swiftly from political imperative to simplistic slogan—readily seized by anyone who wants to justify this or that variety of writing. I am therefore not out to question what Carla Kaplan describes as the "established feminist paradigm of voice," but rather to suggest with her that "we need a more nuanced theory of 'voice'" that accounts for its complex contexts and strategies of articulation (16, 147). How can a cry feed into a critical utterance? How do certain mobile narratives shape a knowing message? What is the crucial conduit between tongue and thought?

Such questions are of no small consequence for feminist theory. In seeking such nuanced understandings of voice, Kaplan concentrates her attention on what she calls an "erotics of talk" in women's literary writing, and rightly calls our attention as well to the trope of erotics in feminist criticism. Here, she claims, the very language of critical writing contests "a strict divide between the erotic, metaphoric, speculative, and celebratory energies" that we find in such essays as Luce Irigaray's "When Our Lips Speak Together" and Hélène Cixous's "Laugh of the Medusa." The erotics of not only French theory, but a broad range of feminist criticism, forms what Kaplan calls "a critical legacy that we need both to recuperate and investigate" (17).

How feminist theory *sounds*, how its audible and aural qualities in turn affect and effect meaning, provides for me the guiding echo in tracing this critical legacy. For I believe that what we continually encounter in feminist theory is hardly some distinctive feminist language, set free at last from patriarchal bondage, but a peculiarly feminist indulgence in the transmutive potential of words, their ability to affirm and question and resist and endlessly suggest meanings, to be used for everything they are worth, and more. In my readings, feminist theory has become a volatile zone where the varied restrictive and generative forces of words bounce and rebound. It has become a place where those of us who are rightly frustrated with the limitations of dominant and normative discourses do something other than create an oppositional language with its own rules and prescriptions.

After all, the feminist critics and theorists I bring together here are volatile, active agents, continually crossing over and beyond linguistic borders, fusing, confusing and refusing their boundaries. They more closely resemble Haraway's "cyborg" than some female subject in search of "feminine" writing. They do not, as Haraway says of her cyborg, "mark time on an Oedipal calendar, attempting to heal the terrible cleavages of gender in an oral symbiotic utopia. . . ." With her, they would argue for "pleasure in the confusion of boundaries and for responsibility in their construction" (*Simians* 150). For me, hearing the O means transgressing certain boundaries. But this process necessarily entails negotiating the multiple meanings and linguistic possibilities that emerge from that transgression. In this sense, listening for possible significations becomes a daring yet cautiously critical act, and one that is rarely ever predictable. Besides, it would be risky, especially these days, to link any single linguistic or cultural phenomenon to the diverse scholarly pursuits that fall under the umbrella of feminism. After all, the expansive field of interdisciplinary feminist theory is lively and contentious, and my own increasingly interdisciplinary engagements with it over the past fifteen years have left me reeling with its shifting perspectives, theoretical twists and turns, its problems and its plentitude. It comes as no surprise that the critical language of feminists should reflect this volatile enterprise.

And yet my project here is hardly exclusively feminist. Nor does the range of writing I deal with fall into some pure category of "feminist theory" untouched by other modes of critical thinking and writing. It melds with other expressions of critical language that often articulate related critical agendas. I am convinced, for instance, that some distinctive qualities of oral, sounded language permeate much postcolonial writing, notably in terms of what Homi Bhabha calls its "affective writing" and "enunciative strategies" that disrupt both the sequence of the written "sentence" and the ways in which colonized people have literally been "sentenced" within history ("Postcolonial Authority" 56). I am also convinced that feminist traversals in language work to open the kinds of sexual and pleasurable writing seized throughout much recent scholarship devoted to gay, lesbian, and queer writing strategies, as Diana Fuss describes the imperative of "using these contested words, use them up, exhaust them, transform them . . . by working the insides of our sexual vocabularies . . ." (7). And the distinctive oral aspects of African-American writing, from the rhythms of poetry to the "soundings" of Houston Baker's own critical prose, permeate multicultural discourse ("Caliban" 390–91). In different and specific contexts, many of these modes of enunciation partake in the unleashing of language and thought announced by postmodern theorists—where linguistic possibilities proliferate through what Derrida calls the "*superabundance* of the signifier" (968), and where we refine what Lyotard calls an increased sensitivity to the "incommensurable" (xxv).

For me, the superabundance and positively incommensurable dimensions of feminist critical writing, echoed within its sonorous language, signal both its possibilities and vulnerabilities. With Susan Griffin, I find myself loving that moment when "language falls short," when "something more" lingers (8). Throughout contemporary theory, there is a sense that any permanent linguistic meaning is elusive, a scenario that might generate all sorts of altercations within language that accrue from the ceaseless mobility of words. Yet all too often for a range of contemporary theorists, the game of hide-and-seek meta-phorically describes this process, and not wanting to secure some false sense of "presence," we are left wandering in a world of veiled, hidden meanings.[4] I read feminist theory with an appreciation for this sense of lingering meaning, but also with an increased sensitivity to the impor-tance of things heard yet unseen. It is not so much a question of concealing or revealing hidden messages, but whether we can enter into a more complicated oral economy where some messages resound with clarity, others are complex and contested, and still others haunt us, as A. S. Byatt would say, like voices heard through the wall, from another room. Meanings are indeed incommensurable within this medium. They echo across the page and in the mind. They generate an abundant audible critique.

And so, with Broumas, I find myself "beginning with O" some-where within the "cave of sound." Yet my meanderings around the O have their own history that has led to the writing of this book. They go back to my interests in orality, and to a wrong turn I once took at the Widner Library at Harvard, stronghold of cultural literacy. While waiting for some texts to be delivered from their home in the stacks, I accidentally found myself in a periodical reading room where I came across a review of Eric Havelock's book, *The Muse Learns to Write: Reflections on Orality and Literacy from Antiquity to the Present*. No small subject, and one that generated much of my reading agenda for the next several years. I take up the subject of orality-literacy contrasts later, but what I do want to note here is the important distinction I have come to draw in my own thinking between orality and what I call the O.

Oral language and culture have a long and rich heritage—complicated, diverse, and endlessly fascinating. One aspect of this subject has proved particularly fascinating to me, and that is the way in which much feminist writing infuses the energies of oral language into a vibrant critical literacy. To call attention to this distinctive phe-nomenon, and especially to its effects—within and beyond feminism—in reshaping critical traditions, I've chosen the configuration of the O. Olga Broumas's poem played no small part in this decision, poetically fusing the body and sounds of language with women's writing. For her, "beginning with O" involves tracing the curves of this language, seizing the bodily contours of writing. For me, hearing the O means, in part, recalling into writing the sounds of oral language, but it also entails a reconsideration of how sound functions in narrative, embodied, poetic, and erotic modes of *literacy*. When Adrienne Rich writes, as a critic, about the urgency to "take that old, material utensil, language, found all about you, blank with familiarity, smeared with daily use, and make it into something more than it says" (*What Is Found There* 84), she is not only describing poetic language, but bringing its energies into critical writing. We need to think about old smeared utensils, about how some things become so familiar they seem blank, about the ways in which language may become blank—all this and more, to follow her message. In other words, we have to read Rich as a critic in much the same way that we read Rich as a poet, listening to the sounding evocations of each word, reading, as Scott says, "for 'the literary'" and all its intimations and interpretations.

To read in this way, to hear the O and all its echoes and resonances, is in part to tap into oral modes of expression, but also to engage some of the most powerful aural qualities of literacy, of the written word. I stress both the distinctly oral and literate properties of the O because I do not want to seem as though I'm uncritically embracing a return to oral language and aligning it with feminine or feminist expression. Like Elizabeth Grosz who, in her book *Volatile Bodies*, worries that her arguments risk "alarming some feminists" who fear that associations of women and body may only enforce patriarchal beliefs, I, too, am concerned that my associations of feminist critical writing and a reverberating, sounding language run similar risks. Exploring these connections should not become either uncritically celebrated or critically taboo forms of inquiry. I am well aware of the dangers of aligning feminist writing with a specific language tradition—oral or literate, gynocentric, maternal, or simply "feminine." But I take these risks because I am also aware of the dangers of shying away from certain subjects because of what they might portend.

And so I use the O with some caution but also with some flair—as a critical sign that refers to orality even as it moves beyond any definition of the oral, that signals the echoes and resonances and sheer motion of words, that ushers us into a "cave of sound" where language, as Rich writes, becomes "something that means more than it says."

But it is risky business, following all these suggestive and excessive significations. Seeking prototypes for her own "polyvocal" critical writing, DuPlessis turns to Virginia Woolf who, in the midst of the Second World War and barely a year before she committed suicide, pondered the language of her critical essays: "'I wish I could invent a new critical method—something swifter and lighter and more colloquial and yet intense: more to the point and less composed: more fluid and following the flight. . . . The old problem: how to keep the flight of the mind, yet be exact. All the difference between the sketch and the finished work. And now dinner to cook. A role. Nightly raids in the east and south coast. 6, 3, 22 people killed nightly'" (*Writer's Diary*

324, *Pink Guitar* vii, 60). The stakes are high in inventing this "new critical method." Woolf must risk writing, on the same page, in the same breath, about the immediacy of dinner and the immediacy of war and death. In similar ways, many feminist critics must risk, on the one hand, being dismissed for using language that is not sufficiently philosophical, analytical, and intellectual. On the other hand, because we enter into the world of critical theory, we also risk being viewed as too theoretical, exclusionary, elitist, and helplessly "high."

Yet these are precisely the risks that so many contemporary feminist critics and theorists are taking. Patricia Williams, trying to speak of the law, becomes willingly lost in language, both fearing and engaging its excessive significations: "My words are confined and undone; I am tangled in gleaming, bubbled words. I hear the sounds of my own voice but they make no sense. . . . I am circled in pretense, entwined in nonsense, tangled in cables and connectors. I speak to the distance of emptiness, I speak in circles and signals, I speak myself into the still" (208–9). Judith Butler, thinking about the terms of her own writing, ponders similar tangles in language: "Is there a pregiven distinction between theory, politics, culture, media? How do those divisions operate to quell a certain intertextual writing that might well generate wholly different epistemic maps? But I am writing here now: is it too late? Can this writing, can any writing, refuse the terms by which it is appropriated even as, to some extent, that very colonizing discourse enables or produces this stumbling block, this resistance?" ("Imitation" 14).

Is it too late? Only if we write in a desperate attempt to seize the perfect words, the pure message untainted by everything else that language intimates. But if we accept that language is always, ceaselessly in flux—that the motion of words is like sound—then we can accept as well that words always mean more than they say. And then it becomes possible to listen for these significations as they move, like waves, in tangled, sometimes fearful, sometimes promising, directions.

For too long, critical theory has been mired in rationalistic approaches to language, as if words were simply a vehicle for offering some faithful representation of some fixed reality. The problem with this approach, as Scott explains, is that "questions about the constructed nature of experience . . . about how one's vision is structured—about language (or discourse) and history—are left aside" ("Evidence" 367). Theory that relies on such a conception and use of language can only work to replicate the stasis of representation and ideas. Hearing the O entails following the sounds of a very different language, words that do not simply reflect a true vision of reality, but show us how that very vision has been constructed, altered, and negotiated through the medium of words. Hearing the O means hearing the process of this continual relation between words and things, sounds and ideas, narrative and history.

Let me turn once again to Olga Broumas, and in the process hint at a subject to which I will return recurrently throughout this book—the urgent need within our culture to reconnect poetry and thought. For without critical language that can evoke both passion and precision, complexity and clarity, reverberation and reason, our attempts at thoughtful critique will follow the already well-worn path of a placid, hopelessly quantified, social scientific prose. Literary language will continue to be siphoned off for the domains of entertainment and reflective self-help treatises. Within the university, the humanities will continue in their state of decline and devaluation, with art flourishing as fetish. Political bravado, feminist or otherwise, will not save us from this scenario. Nor am I persuaded that the brave new world of technological media and the silver screens of cinema, television, and the computer will somehow rescue us from the demise of literacy and print culture, returning us to a revitalized condition of orality and global understanding.[5] Any medium can be manipulated and maligned; few have been so insidiously controlled by the market economy as has the technological word.

But a passionate attention to language, to its sounding and signifying possibilities, might help turn us elsewhere—perhaps away from the glitzy and fast-paced information culture we have become, and toward a slower, more thoughtful, more intense engagement with the written word. Perhaps we need to learn, again, how to read and write, but with a fierce attention to the suggestive sounds of words. Broumas explains her own project this way:

> I am a woman committed to
> a politics
> of transliteration, the methodology
>
> of a mind
> stunned at the suddenly
> possible shifts of meaning—for which
> like amnesiacs
>
> in a ward on fire, we must
> find words
> or burn. (24)

She begins her task by tracing the language of a "curviform alphabet," "beginning with O." I'll begin by following its critical curves around these questions: What is the "politics of transliteration" at work in so much feminist scholarship? What are the "possible shifts in meaning" that this turn in language generates?

This book begins with a poem and ends with a chapter on poetic literacy. Yet it is about contemporary feminist critics and theorists. In a sense, its scope is fairly circumscribed. But like the language of poetry, the language tapped by these writers signals a move beyond the page, into the spaces where written words begin to sound, and move. Where those sounds lead marks my haunt.

1

Vocal Critics

Introductions to books can be revealing, especially books of feminist criticism. Nancy K. Miller, in *Getting Personal*, entitles her Preface "Feminist Confessions: The Last Degrees Are the Hardest," where she writes: "Most of the chapters of this book were, at least originally, occasional. I have never really understood why occasional writing is held to be a deconsidered genre. . . . (Actually, I do understand, but I don't share the prejudice. I prefer the gossipy grain of situated writing to the academic sublime)" (11). Introducing her work *Borderlands / La Frontera*, Gloria Anzaldúa describes her palpable engagement with "words, my passion for the daily struggle to render them concrete in the world and on paper, to render them flesh . . ." (Preface). Approaching the corporeal dimensions of writing a bit differently, Judith Butler prefaces her work, *Bodies That Matter*, by describing a question continually asked of her: "In the recent past, the question was repeatedly formulated to me this way: 'What about the materiality of the body, *Judy?*' I took it that the addition of 'Judy' was an effort to dislodge me from the more formal 'Judith' and to recall me to a bodily life that could not be theorized away" (ix). What kinds of writing and bodies might be dislodged, assembled and reassembled? Eve Sedgwick introduces her collection of critical essays, *Tendencies*, by describing not only their "queer" subjects, but the various "queer" and "crossed" forms of writing she engages: "the autobiographical narrative, the performance piece, the atrocity story, the polemic, the prose essay that quotes poetry, the obituary" (xiv). The desire for this mosaic of prosy, embodied, theoretical, autobiographical, polemical, poetic essays would seem to fuel the passion of much feminist criticism. Rachael DuPlessis opens her book *The Pink Guitar* with these words: "I began to write essays, with an abrupt startled need, in 1978; the first was 'Psyche, or Wholeness' . . . in which elements of guarded, yet frank autobiography, textual analysis, and revisionary myth-making suddenly fused into a demanding voice, with a mix of ecstatic power over cultural materials and mourning for the place of the female in culture. The multiple pressures of living out feminist thinking led me again and again to this non-objective, polyvocal prose . . ." (vii).

Almost as if commenting on these messages about feminist critical writing, Ruth-Ellen Boetcher Joers and Elizabeth Mittman introduce their collection, *The Politics of the Essay: Feminist Perspectives*, by wondering if "the essay—with its openness, its accessibility, its sense of initiated dialogue, its emphasis on the particular and the concrete, its stress on dynamic process—could become an alternative form for feminist critical writing . . ." (20). Something in me wants to reply, "What do you mean *could* become an alternative form?" We seem already to be very much there, and yet, where exactly is this site of writing, and what are its writerly contours and contexts? Responding both analytically and self-consciously to such questions, various critics have described this "alternative" mode in different terms—as distinctly postmodern, or reflective of multicultural traditions, as just plain personal or enticingly queer, or simply "feminine" and appropriately intimate. I want to account for it as a reworking of critical language instigated by the emergence of sound within the written word, and the effects produced by the oral and aural reverberations of language as they infuse writing and thought. For what the introductions to all these books reveal is the intense attention their authors devote to their own critical language, and the way this intensity builds from a sonorous and somatic engagement with words—gossipy and fleshy, dialogic, performative, polyvocal.

I have grown especially interested in the twists and turns of critical language since this genre of writing has itself become the site for questioning and contesting so many assumptions about language. The conspicuous emergence of critical theory during the last three decades—to the delight of some and disgust of others—signals a wide-ranging inquiry into the very linguistic grounds we stand on. Words, metaphors, and signifiers churn away in this so-called linguistic turn of events, where language shapes the very theory that examines the construction and effects of language. Across the disciplines, the language that feeds critical traditions—in the diverse registers of philosophy, science, law, the humanities, and social sciences—has become conspicuously unstable material, vulnerable to deconstruction and an accompanying analysis of the cultural forces that give it shape and legitimacy. Discourse has moved to the forefront of our intellectual probings. In many ways, discourse has become *the* subject of theory.

With all this talk about language and discourse, it comes as no surprise that the very notion of literacy has grown into a hotly contested topic. Calls for reclaiming literacy—in terms of both writing skills and a

written record of knowledge—have attracted more than their fair share
of attention in recent years, especially from conservative writers bent on
preserving the kind of standardized language and cohesive knowledge
described by E. D. Hirsch in his best-selling book *Cultural Literacy: What
Every American Should Know*. All the while, within the terrain of
scholarly critique, which hardly seems to sell at all these days, literacy
and literate traditions are neither standardized nor stable. Wlad
Godzich, for example, in his book *The Culture of Literacy*, responds to
those who would insist on a fairly standardized literacy by arguing that
we must be aware of the "multiplicity of functions that language
performs" (5). He describes "difference-sensitive theory" as that which
recognizes a "cry," not some universalizing and cohesive language, but
those proliferating utterances that "can only sound and resound" (26).

Writing more specifically about such sounding literacy, Houston
Baker argues that African-American scholarly writing should make
room for "vernacular rhythms" and poetic "sounds." Enacting this
language in his own criticism, Baker explains that his purpose is not to
replace European traditions of literacy with Afrocentric ones, but to
produce what he calls "supraliteracy," the opening of spaces "*within
linguistic territories*" that would augur the rearrangement of literacy
itself. The result is an exceptionally mixed mode of critical writing,
language that incorporates lines from Shakespeare and Ralph Ellison,
sounds from gorillas and philosophical musings from Jacques Derrida,
not to mention Baker's own theoretical abstractions often rendered in
rhythmic, poetic cadences—as when he offers this jazzy description of
supraliteracy as an event that "changes a dualistic Western joke and
opens a space for the sui generis and liberating sound of the formerly
yoked" (382). Shunning the styles associated with a conventional critical
writing, or for that matter with a rebellious sounding orality, Baker's
supraliteracy is nonetheless doggedly critical. He keeps his ear tuned
for the workings of language and thought.

Baker and Godzich, as we shall see, are hardly the only theorists
who approach concepts of written language by shifting our attention to
the dynamics of the oral. But in interesting ways, they—along with
Hirsch—help me frame my own reading of feminist theory and its
sonorous linguistic conduits. For I sense that something is happening
with the language of feminist theory, a kind of discursive shift in the
midst of the linguistic turn, one which opens spaces "within linguistic
territories" for sound and for the "resounding" meanings that have
peculiar and crucial bearings on feminist thought. Hirsch does not even
mention feminist thought in his claims about cultural literacy (though
he includes the word "feminism" under the letter "f" in his list of terms

that "Literate Americans Know," preceded by the entry "female of the species is more deadly than the male"). Godzich acknowledges that his book contains absolutely "no engagement with feminism" (33) because his early experiences with the feminist movement have made him question its racial biases. Meanwhile Baker, who elsewhere devotes important critical attention especially to African-American women writers, here understandably focuses entirely on the racial dimensions of a sounding language.

Thus the frame that these three very different critics construct both sets up parameters and, at the same time but in different ways, ignores the large and looming questions surrounding feminism and language. As a result, our conceptions of cultural literacy are not only woefully incomplete, but miss the opportunity to gauge the effects of feminist writing that enacts the very kinds of sounds identified by Baker and Godzich. And so I readily use their frame as an entrance into feminist linguistic territory, a passageway that leads through the looking glass and into the audible sphere of feminist theory. Let me begin by suggesting that this enactment of sound in writing works like a voice.

⑥

In women's speech, as in their writing, that element which never stops resonating . . . that element is the song. . . . Why this privileged relationship with the voice?

—Hélène Cixous ("Laugh" 251)

I guess the same invitation made me want my essay "rendered" in the writerly sense—wrought, maybe verging on wrought up. . . . (I remember how much I cheered up . . . when I realized one result was that I could start with a sentence in iambic pentameter. . . .) I wanted to make it inescapable that the piece *was* writerly.

—Eve Sedgwick ("Against Epistemology" 134)

What is it about voice and writing, vocalization and writerliness, that so distinctively fuels much feminist theory? In this opening chapter, I want to ponder the connections between oral sounds and written words, the ways in which voice can insinuate itself in writing. Critical theorists, after all, are highly literate creatures—and often notoriously "writerly" creatures as well. How might we turn an ear toward the aural tenor of this writing, listening for messages in the very suggestive and complicating sounds of language?

I pose these questions because I believe that we need to understand feminist critical writing as something more than personal or subjective, and as something that unfolds more complexly and more sensuously than voice erupting from silence. Not that I object to these terms, or that I discount the historical reality of women's diverse and long-enforced silences within literate traditions. But feminist writing, especially as it takes shape within the contemporary scene of criticism and theory, is complicated, critically complicated, by the mixture of different orders and modes of language. And voice, too, is a complicated concept. Voice can proclaim, as Cixous insists women's voices must when they infuse writing and sustain "the power moving us" ("Laugh" 251). But voice also has a way of insinuating itself in writing—as Sedgwick's "writerly" iambic pentameter line alerts us not so much to her ideas, but as she explains, to the "unacknowledged codependency between the institutions and disciplines of humanistic thought, even the chastest of them, and the ostensibly marginalized practice of the florid writerliness of many of their founders, catalysts, and celebrities" ("Against Epistemology" 135).

I get Sedgwick's message, but more than that, I hear other meanings evoked in this passage: her choice, superlative term, "chastest," urges me to conjoin the notions of sexual and linguistic purity, to wonder if this purity has been linked to institutional and humanistic thought that strives for communication through pure, untainted language. Her own carefully paced sentence neatly combines two clauses, but then complicates their meanings: a reader must search for messages not only by putting all the parts together, but following the suggestions and echoes of related ideas—from "codependency" to "catalysts" and "celebrities." I find myself considering, and reconsidering, exactly who is dependent on what, pondering the divergent claims of chaste and florid language, disciplined and florid thought. And my own thinking begins to move—to subjects hardly unrelated to Sedgwick's claim, but different from the particular topics she discusses.

I recall, for example, the notions of "writerly" and "readerly" language described by Roland Barthes, where to be "writerly"—far from Sedgwick's notion—is to be authoritative and definitive in one's use of writing, but where to be "readerly" is to write precisely for the "plural" meanings of words. The vocal quality of such writing is unmistakable in Barthes, who suggests that even determinate modes of writing invite us to "listen to the text as an iridescent exchange carried on by multiple voices, on different wavelengths and subject from time to time to a sudden *dissolve*, leaving a gap that enables the utterance to shift from one point of view to another, without warning: the writing is set up across this tonal instability . . . which makes it a glistening texture of ephemeral origins" (*S/Z* 41–42). Perhaps responding to such "sudden *dissolve*," I shift my own point of view to Virginia Woolf, thinking about her novel *The Waves*, her eventual suicide by drowning—and recall how she captured her own ambivalent feelings about the great repositories of such texts when, standing in front of the university libraries of England, she pondered "how unpleasant it is to be locked out" while also reflecting "how it is worse perhaps to be locked in" (*A Room of One's Own* 24). Am I reading too much into Sedgwick's sentence? Or am I simply reading it for all its "tonal instability," its sounding, rebounding suggestibility? Am I being excessively oral, or am I tuning into the waverings of the written word?

We know that poetry and novels, not to mention other modes of literary writing, have long been infused with the energies of oral, sounding language, in myriad traditions and contexts.[1] But the specific genres of critical and theoretical writing have largely kept the audible resonances of language at bay. As Joan Scott, describing conventional traditions for social scientific prose, says, "Knowledge is gained through vision; vision is a direct apprehension of a world of transparent objects . . . writing is then put at its service. . . . Writing is reproduction, transmission . . ." ("Evidence" 365–66). In short, disciplined writing should be transparent; thoughts must be made clear—as in, "I *see* what you mean." Sounds and metaphors that blur this clarity must be sharpened, focused, "put in the service" of what we can be seen and known. Thus scholarly precision, critical insight, theoretical mastery.

Then again, what might happen if knowledge and writing were not so tightly, exclusively linked to vision? Donna Haraway, writing about "Situated Knowledges," wants to hold onto to vision, which she describes as a "much maligned sensory system in feminist discourse" (*Simians* 188). And yet the kind of vision she has in mind resembles more the changing, refracting qualities of light that Scott, as I described in the opening of this book, associates with the dimming and reflective medium of language. Instead of clear, focused, universal vision, Haraway urges us to hone in on "partial perspective." Her examples of such vision actually run the gamut of sensory experience:

These are lessons which I learned in part walking with my dogs and wondering how the world looks without a fovea and very few retinal cells for colour vision, but with a huge neural processing and sensory area for smells. It is a lesson available from photographs of how the world looks to the compound eyes of an insect, or even from the camera eye of a spy satellite or the digitally transmitted signals of space probe–perceived differences "near" Jupiter that have been transformed into coffee table colour photographs. (*Simians* 190)

There is vision here, to be sure, refracted through the eyes of an insect, differently shaded through the eyes of her dogs, who are of course seen through the eyes of Haraway. But then we also have her dogs smelling their way to knowledge of the world. And we have those "digitally transmitted signals" from Jupiter, coming to us via a translation of sound waves into numbers. Is all this vision, or vision negotiated through an assortment of sensory devices? And if Haraway's dogs are like mine, then there is the question of their barking, their vocal response to stimuli, visual or otherwise, not to mention their intense sense of hearing virtually everything that moves—all of which play a part in the sensory ways we come to know our worlds.

And then there is the question of Haraway's own critical language, its lively motion, its relentless pace. Describing her frustration with philosophers who believe in a fixed scientific objective vision, she writes:

Of course, my designation of [such philosophers] is probably just a reflection of residual disciplinary chauvinism from identifying with historians of science and too much time spent with a microscope in early adulthood in a kind of disciplinary pre-oedipal and modernist poetic moment when cells seemed to be cells and organisms, organisms. *Pace*, Gertrude Stein. But then came the law of the father and its resolution of the problem of objectivity, solved by always already absent referents, deferred signifieds, split subjects, and the endless play of signifiers. Who wouldn't grow up warped? (*Simians* 184)

Something about Haraway's prose *sounds* like it does indeed generate from a pre-oedipal and poetic moment. She seems as willingly "tangled" in her language as Patricia Williams is when she describes being caught up in "cables and connectors," in "bubbled words" (208–9). To be "warped," in this sense, is to realize that your language always means more than you say. My question for Haraway is this: How does one recall and engage these excessive meanings, the "absent referents, deferred signifieds . . . the endless play of signifiers"? Don't words themselves echo the sounds and meanings of other absent or deferred words? When, for instance, I read "*Pace*, Gertrude Stein," I can almost hear some of Stein's own "endless play of signifiers" in Haraway's very language. It is as if a kind of rhythmic, endlessly suggestive poetic language pulses within Haraway's critical prose. I can hear its beat, and *through these sounds*, I can *think* of subjects that are absent, deferred, now recalled and tangled into what I read, into what is written.

We might say that the sounds of Stein's rhythmic and repitious writing haunt Haraway's critical prose. Indeed we might simply say that sound itself haunts the written word.

ⓑ

> Even displaced, set aside or considered as a remainder, enunci-
> ation cannot be dissociated from the system of statements. . . .
> [W]e can distinguish between writing's effort to master the
> "voice" that it cannot be but without which it nevertheless cannot
> exist, on the one hand, and the illegible returns of voices cutting
> across statements and moving like strangers through the house of
> language, like imagination.
>
> —Michel de Certeau (159)

When I read Haraway, when I read myriad expressions of feminist theory, I sense something oral and vocal wandering around in their sentences, "moving" very much "like strangers through the house of language." Of course the oral qualities of language have always become audible whenever writers exploit the sounding properties of the written word—in varied literary and especially poetic modes of writing, as I've suggested, and often as well in conversational and dialogic prose, even unintentionally in writing that strives to be transparent but where words and phrases speak their own suggestive sounds in spite of the text's purported meanings.

But orality itself is a topic whose history and ramifications extend far beyond the written word—into the study of diverse oral cultures, and into diverse theories about the different registers of spoken and written language, oral and literate practices. Consider Walter Ong's pivotal study of *Orality and Literacy*, which synthesized an enormous amount of research devoted to the distinctly oral language practices of such cultures and groups as the Aborigines of Australia, narrative poets in parts of eastern Europe, the Lakota Sioux in North America, African-American preachers and gospel singers, the Luba in Zaire, medieval troubadours throughout Europe, and the Homeric Greeks. Synthesizing this research, Ong developed a list of the peculiar "psychodynamics" of orality sustained largely through the powers of sound in cultures without written texts to store information. Among these characteristics of oral language are its additive, aggregative, and redundant qualities (contrasted with the sparse linear construction of writing) that foster rich oral expression; its agonistically toned expression and its empa-

thetic and participatory qualities that reflect the immediacy of inter-
personal relations (contrasted with the distancing that writing tends to
foster); its immersion in present events and its closeness to human
experience (contrasted with written facts or ideas divorced from human
activity). The effects of such language are to promote thought that is
situational rather than abstract, that is tied to immediate events rather
than the product of distanced, analytic reflection and speculation. Again
and again, Ong emphasizes the peculiar effects of sound as a linguistic
medium, one that stores information and continually reshapes that
information through rhythmic vocal utterances. As such, sounding
language bears a peculiar and crucial relationship to thought, which
becomes a dynamic product of sounding language.

Numerous scholars have variously echoed Ong's conclusions
even while revising and adjusting his arguments.[2] Some of the more
striking examples of this investigation into oral-literate contrasts would
include Eric Havelock's work that links writing with the inception of
philosophy and abstract thought in classical Greek culture; Jack
Goody's arguments about how writing shaped modern social and
bureaucratic systems, and about the "interface" of orality and literacy in
diverse cultures; Ruth Finnegan's detailed observations on the complexity of communication and thought in numerous indigenous
cultures; Marshall McLuhan's intriguing speculations about the oral
dimensions of contemporary media technology; Deborah Tannen's
linguistic analysis of the oral-literate continuum in conversation; John
Miles Foley's investigations of oral performance; Jonathan Boyarin's
collection of essays, which address the interactions of orality and
textuality in the reading process; and in a more theoretical vein, Michel
de Certeau's analysis of our "Scriptural Economy" and the ways in
which it is permeated with the residual sounds of orality.

Could any or many of these theories about the distinctive qualities
of oral language bear on the sounding qualities of feminist critical
language? I would cautiously suggest that they do, and that what I call
"hearing the O" relies to a large extent on the capacity to develop a
sense for the sounds and nuances of the spoken word. But in reading
feminist theory, we have obviously crossed over from oral to literate
territory; and in listening for sounds *in writing*, we are obviously
dealing with a peculiar intersection of the oral and literate. Thus I've
found myself drawn to one particular and particularly fascinating
dimension of research devoted to oral-literate contrasts: the effects of
orality as it feeds, as is seeps into and permeates, the written word.

I believe that such a concern is of no small consequence in feminist
theory, yet our awareness of the possible "residual sounds of orality" in

written language remains unconnected in any sustained way with the feminist inquiries into gender-based language differences, topics surveyed in such recent anthologies as *The Feminist Critique of Language* and *The Women and Language Debate*. It is not that such connections have gone completely unnoticed. Ong, for instance, has speculated that European women's exclusion from learned Latin for well over a thousand years must have influenced the style of women writers particularly as they contributed to the development of the novel and made it "more like a conversation than a platform performance" (160). In very different contexts, one can hardly miss the oral forces at play in Kristeva's notion of the "semiotic disposition" of language ("From One Identity"). Recently, Katie King has explored what she calls the "politics of the oral and the written" to argue for the inclusion of poetry, song, and story within the genres of feminist theory, and argues further that we need to pay attention to varied "writing technologies" that inform feminist and cultural literacies.[3] And as I have insisted throughout, myriad feminist claims about voice are rooted both metaphorically and materially in the oral resonances of language.

Yet what if we are dealing specifically with the language and genres of critical writing, with the sharp analysis and hefty abstractions of theory? I want to suggest that some appreciation for how sound works in oral language can help us approach this question by turning our sensory antennae to what is audible rather than purely visible in critical language and thought. For instead of looking at words on a page, people in oral cultures talk and listen, a distinction far more revolutionary than it may at first seem because of the remarkably different physical and psychological effects of sound and sight. While sight inevitably entails some distancing between observer and observed, the environment of sound tends to be one of immersion.[4] Some oralists suggest that sight becomes a dominant mode of sensation in literate cultures, and dissection and analysis accordingly become dominant means of response and thought; whereas in oral cultures, sound functions as a primary mode of sensation, and thought and analysis evolve through the continual retellings of narratives (Ong 72, Havelock 111).

But the argument can turn. The peculiar modes of sensation and thought associated with sound can blend into writing, as on a mobius strip, and language built on visual distance can turn into one of immersion, resonance, suggestibility. In his most recent study of oral works, for example, John Miles Foley advocates a "spectrum model" for understanding the connections and complicity of oral and literate language. Following this model, he suggests, we might study language ranging "from the now rare situations in which writing has played no part whatsoever through the myriad intermediate cases where oral tradition and literacy intertwine in fascinating ways and on to the works composed by literate authors that nonetheless owe some debt to an originative oral tradition" (210–11).[5]

Adopting a similar tone, Eric Havelock, in an essay written just before his death in 1988, suggested that the myriad studies of orality to emerge during the past twenty years have not only redirected us to the spoken word, but have "provoked closer attention to its counterpart, the book, the printed text, the written word." Expanding on the significance of this move, he continued: "Far from going back to orality, what we can be invited to explore in depth are the new possibilities of literacy, a literacy of readers of communication by print, rather than literacy by voice" ("Equation" 18).

Among such studies he mentions are Elizabeth Eisenstein's investigations into the effects of print in reshaping culture, and also what he calls "the ways in which modern philosophies in their speculations have also occasionally brushed against the oralists' question, having viewed, perhaps reluctantly, the presence of oralism in the modern mind" ("Equation" 19). His specific references are to the Derridean "distrust" and deconstruction of writing, Heidegger's search "for hidden and deeper meanings concealed in textualized statements," Wittgenstein's movement away from a conception of "language as the instrument of logical clarity," and J. L. Austin's study of speech acts and the "syntax of performative speech" (17–19). To these I would add Foucault's ideas about the incessant "buzzing of discourse," Bakhtin's theories of the "dialogic" qualities of writing, Barthes's notion of *Writing Degree Zero* and its ceaseless "signifying" potential and "plentitude" (WDZ 48, S/Z 216)—his zero echoing the same sounds of the O that I discern in writing. These very sounds invite us "to listen to the text," as Barthes says, "as an iridescent exchange carried on by multiple voices" (S/Z 41–42).

In my own attempts to come to terms with what Havelock calls the "presence of oralism in the modern mind" (we might more accurately say the postmodern mind), the ideas of Michel de Certeau can particularly help to put us in touch with the residual traces of orality in writing, and to follow the actual "enactment" of oral language as it affects word and meaning. In his essays "The Scriptural Economy" and "Quotations of Voices," de Certeau explores the varied institutional effects of writing (isolation, classification, systematization, capital, the modern city, technocratic society, legal regulation), and the residual effects of orality as the spoken word "insinuate[s] itself into a text" as a "reminiscence in the scriptural economy, a disturbing sound from a different tradition, and a pre-text for interminable interpretive productions" (155).

Yet these two orders of language—the scriptural and the vocal—are not, de Certeau insists, definitively opposed to each other. Far from that, within the scriptural economy they mutually affect each other, and in varied ways. At times, voice remains purely exterior to writing, such that the resulting discourse continually attempts to "multiply products that substitute for an absent voice . . ." (161). At other times, there emerges what de Certeau calls a "space for voices" in the text, where enunciation "disturbs and interferes with syntax . . ." (162). For example, he considers these different effects of sound in literary and scholarly writing: "The literary text is modified by becoming the ambiguous depth in which sounds that cannot be reduced to a meaning move about" (162); "In scholarly writing, it is nothing other than the return of voices through which the social body 'speaks' in quotation, sentence fragments, the tonalities of 'words,' the sounds they make" (163).

Of course I am precisely interested in this phenomenon of what happens in *scholarly* writing—this "return of voices," the way they move around, disturb, interfere, remain ambiguous. And I find myself especially drawn to the idea that they function as an "enunciation," an "enactment" of what is otherwise written about or described from some distance. For my sense is that while varied contemporary theorists have described this phenomenon, feminist theory is distinctive in the ways in which it enunciates these voices, enacts this language. When sounds enact meanings, de Certeau understands them as a "practice." I understand feminist theory as such a "practice," or to recall Rachael DuPlessis's evocative terms:

The practice of anguage. The anguish of language. The anger of language. (165)

When orality "insinuates itself" in the scriptural domain, voice becomes not some revolutionary cry that overthrows a staid and systematic literacy, but instead emerges as volatile, transitory, potentially disturbing and transforming practices *within* language that keep words and their references on the move. Thus "anguish" insinuates itself, through its very sound, into "language." Thus "language," echoing "anguish," is itself insinuated with "anger." Thus one word, one thought, resonates with and into another. Through sound, words move.

⑥

Talk to me
Three words
moving with heavy feet
across the open spaces

                        —Margaret Randall (*Dancing* 35)

If voice can insinuate itself in written language, then I would evoke Randall's invitation, "Talk to me," as urging us to make some very specific oral moves on the page and all its potential open spaces. For it is precisely these kinds of moves, I believe, that are enacted throughout feminist discourse. For example, Bakhtin's ideas about dialogic language—the "living utterance" that "cannot fail to brush up against thousands of living dialogic threads," which "cannot fail to become an active participant in social dialogue" (276)—shares more directly with the dialogic powers of oral communication than, say, Derrida's more abstract deconstructions of writing. But compared to either of these theorists, the lyrical prose of Hélène Cixous actually brings to, seizes within, critical writing the very "phonic and oral dimensions of language" that she describes: "But look, our seas are what we make of them, full of fish or not, opaque or transparent. . . . Heterogeneous, yes" (*Laugh* 260). Bakhtin and Derrida write compellingly about the event; Cixous enacts it. Similarly, Patricia Williams's own critical narratives directly engage the kind of dialogic exchange that Bakhtin associates with the novel, making space for a critical heteroglossia, a critical social dialogue, in her analysis of the law:

"'But what's the book *about*?' my sister asks, thumping her leg against the chair impatiently.

'Howard Beach, polar bears, and food stamps,' I snap back. 'I am interested in the way in which legal language flattens and confines in absolutes the complexity of meaning inherent in any given problem . . .'" (6).

These kinds of expression—intense engagements with sound and rhythm, with dialogue, with the unfolding narrative of thought, "Howard Beach, polar bears, and food stamps"—mark the residual effects of oral language *within critical writing*. They share much with related critiques of logocentrism, but there is a direct engagement here—what de Certeau calls a "practice" and what DuPlessis would surely nod to as a distinctly "feminist practice"—that marks Williams's writing as different. We know that contemporary theorists talk endlessly about language, but what I've come to recognize more and more is that feminist theorists are conspicuous for actually *talking* that language in their writing, for making the "practice" of language so conspicuous in their critical thought.

And yet, there is also something about the oral that might well make feminist scholars uneasy. We are, after all, a highly literate group with strong, albeit different, connections to the written word. What's more, orality may signal certain danger zones within feminist criticism and theory—such as a lost realm of maternal origins that might be idealized as refuge from a paternalistic world, or a lost feminine language existing outside the phallic symbolic order. For many feminist scholars, the study of orality is simply foreign territory, more the terrain of anthropologists and folklorists than critics and theorists. For some, to enter into the worlds of oral tradition may risk the appropriation of cultures not our own; for others, aligning all women with oral language runs the risk of essentializing women and the language we claim.

All of these hesitations seem plausible to me, though hardly sufficient to warrant turning away from such a rich and suggestive field of inquiry. As I have said and will continue to say throughout this book, the feminist critics I bring together here delve into the process of transformation, not reclamation. Orality in their writing does not mark some distinctive order of language, but instead becomes a vehicle for instigating changes in language from within, through the medium of sound. This is not a story of return, but of rupture and reinvention. Besides, oral language holds no golden key to liberation, offers no absolute refuge from any variety of beliefs and ideas and ideologies— from matrifocal to patriarchal, fascist to anarchist, empirical to postmodern—that language may encode. The kinds of epistemologies shaped through oral narrative can be as diverse as those encoded in the stories of Mwindo in the African Mwindo epic, the quests of Ulysses in early Greek oral epic, the spiderwoman stories of certain Native American groups, or any number of filmic narratives that unfold in movie theaters. Engaging the dynamics of voice will not necessarily return us to a world more sensitive to the experiences and imaginations of women any more than literacy will inevitably take us down the road of patriarchy.

Yet oral language is a particular kind of conduit that produces peculiar effects both on its own and within the parameters of writing. How this happens within feminist critical writing is, I believe, a story all its own—with its distinctive characteristics, effects, ramifications. Indeed the very concepts of orality and sound themselves only partly account for a more complex range of sensory suggestion that permeates feminist theory. As I suggested earlier when reading passages from

Haraway's prose, its rhythm and movement draw us at once into intense visual, aural, and kinetic modes of thought—as we follow the visible path of words on the page, hear their sounds, try to keep pace with their motion: "But then came the law of the father and its resolution of the problem of objectivity, solved by always already absent referents, deferred signifieds, split subjects, and the endless play of signifiers." For me, the sounding qualities of this language—its rhythms, alliterative patterns, its sheer rhetorical flair, what Sedgwick would call its "writerliness"—provide a kind of primary conduit for multiple sensory energies, not the least of which is the very expanded, refracted notion of vision that Haraway seeks to theorize.

At the beginning of this chapter, I referred to Nancy K. Miller's preference for what she calls "the gossipy grain of situated writing to the academic sublime" (11). As someone with a fondness for both styles of language, I can sense how Miller's own prose keeps moving between these two alternative modes, almost as if one is haunting the other. I often become fixated on its own "gossipy grain," an almost tactile quality to Miller's words and narrative that helps me feel my way along an incident, only to find myself ultimately caught up in the sublimity of critical thought, populated by voices in the house of theory.

For example, Miller describes an incident at an academic conference on feminist theory, where everyone commenced to claim, speak from, and speak for specific ethnic and racial identities. First, Miller relates, one speaker "exhorted Jewish women to identify themselves (take back their names and their noses) and wondered aloud from the platform, aggressively, polemically, why Jewish (better yet, Yiddish), female-authored texts were not taught in Women's Studies courses alongside Chicana, Native American, etc. works as 'ethnic' or 'minority' literature (which is a fair enough question)." Then another speaker replies, "equally polemically and upping the ante, that Jews had no right to speak of oppression or marginality since, unlike blacks, they could 'choose to pass.'" Then another, Miller continues, "rose from the audience to observe that six million of them seemed to have failed to exercise that option." And then another of the panelists "urged the audience to remember their Palestinian sisters, who were not with us, and whose men were dying." In response to all of which, Miller writes: "I sat there, in silent shock at the turn this politically correct occasion was taking, not saying anything, and waiting for it to be over" (96).

The "gossipy grain" here is unmistakable, and so are all its sounding, oral properties: there is the translation, in writing, of spoken voices; there is one speaker who "wondered aloud" from the platform; there's what oralists would call the agonistically toned expression and the participatory exchange that characterize oral communication; there are rhetorical exhortations and urgings. In short, the sounds of language permeate this "gossipy" writing, even the empty echo of Miller's own "silent shock," her "not saying anything" in response. And yet, the "academic sublime" lingers, as we wait for Miller to say something, critically, about the event—to think about it in writing, to produce theory. And so this sentence follows: "What was there, really, to say once the structure of competing oppressions had been put in place in those terms?"

Keeping in mind that all these voices are emerging at a feminist theory conference, we can rightly ask what theory indeed lurks here. For Miller is very much working toward the articulation of theory. She proceeds to contemplate what it means for her to be Jewish, what it might mean for her to "speak 'as a Jew,'" why she really does not want to assume that "rhetoric of identity" even though she is, in fact, both Jewish and feminist. She decides that she does not want to be involved in "signing" the quotations she reads from her writings, that she would prefer to let "readers read for me—which meant their placing, identifying, and worst of all, perhaps, misreading me. . . ." And so, at last, we arrive at something like the "academic sublime," but already so infected with gossip and voice that the two modes insinuate themselves in each other in Miller's final ponderings:

> The questions before us in critical theory might go something like this: can we imagine a self-representational practice—for feminism—that is not recontained by the pre-constituted tropes of representativity? How do the cultural and political constraints that provide the context for our discussion police and shortcircuit their effects? (97–98)

Her language has suddenly taken flight from the "gossipy grain of situated writing" to the hefty abstractions of theory: we are now caught up in "self-representational practices," "pre-constituted tropes," "representativity" itself. And yet something about the words "pre-constituted," "political restraints," and "police" (is their alliteration intentional?) brings us back to the matter of voice—not some liberated voice speaking this or that ethnic position, but quite the opposite: the way such a voice may already be policed, determined, made to speak in a certain sanctioned fashion. After the emergence of so many voices, what we arrive at here, at last, is a rather resounding critique of voices, self-representational practices, the whole issue of representation itself. And Miller's own voice—as a critic, as a theorist—hardly shouts out from the page, but instead instigates, and is itself instigated by, sounding moves within her own writing and thinking.

Is she engaging in gossip or in the academic sublime? What other gossipy sounds might be absent here, or deferred, or signified elsewhere? If the academic sublime is haunted by such gossipy voices, how, in turn, might academic gossip be haunted by sublime writing? If we can engage these questions as we read Miller (and she does deliberately invite our readings rather than stamp messages with her own signature), if we can follow the residual sounds of her words, then we are beginning to hear the O. We are beginning to get in touch not with some voice emerging from silence, but with the sounds and voices that haunt feminist critical writing.

He said, I am the voice of one crying in the wilderness, Make straight the way of the Lord. . . .

—John 1.23

I am perception and knowledge, uttering a Voice by means of Thought. [I] am the real voice. I cry out in everyone, and they know that a seed dwells within.

—*Gnostic Gospels* (66)

In my initial drafts of this book, I had hardly imagined turning to the gnostic gospels as a way of discussing voice in contemporary feminist theory. Now, such a turn seems an apt way to bring this first chapter to a close. It also brings us back again to the topic of cultural literacy—that hotly contested field of language and knowledge—and to a reconsideration of the ways in which writing practices often remain "transparent," to use Scott's term ("Experience," 368), and work only to confirm existing ideas and thought paradigms. How do certain modes of language—such as objective description—remain "transparent," while other kinds of language—erotic, passionate, poetic—are said to be charged with predetermined meanings? Indeed how might the texts of early Christianity be read as documenting such contested notions of language?

I am drawn to Elaine Pagels's studies of the gnostic gospels as an example of the way certain modes of language construct the discourse of early Christianity, and the way other kinds of language are ultimately suppressed—all of which turns out to be of no small concern to feminists. Hers is an investigation into the origins of early Christianity, but it is also an exposure of the means through which those who controlled the production of texts also suppressed certain kinds and qualities of language.

As Pagels details her critical narrative, four books in the New Testament—the gospels of Matthew, Mark, Luke, and John—are accepted by millions of people as relating the words and messages of Jesus Christ. But these are by no means the only "testaments" of what Jesus Christ had to say. At least some fifty-two texts—retrieved from a buried urn that was accidentally discovered in upper Egypt—contain various other gospels, secret teachings, narratives and poems that were attributed to Jesus Christ or his disciples. Recent textual scholarship has shown that these texts are translations of writings that circulated during the first century A.D., around the same time as had the now approved gospels of the New Testament. Yet by 200 A.D., these other gospels had been almost entirely suppressed by the bishops and priests who controlled the early institution of Christianity. Why?

Pagels's fascinating account of the gnostic gospels gives us all sorts of information about these texts and possible reasons for their suppression. Generally, the gnostic texts were denounced because they contained varied kinds of information that was deemed unacceptable and "unorthodox." In some, Christ is portrayed as a figure more inter-ested in illusion and enlightenment than in sin and repentance, more eastern than western in his teachings. In another, the story of the Garden of Eden is told from the viewpoint of the serpent. In others, we read of the power of the Mother and feminine elements in the divine. Yet remarkable as it may seem, these diverse messages contained in the gnostic gospels were denounced as heretical and suppressed by priests and bishops in the space of a mere century. To a large extent, as Pagels documents in her third chapter of *The Gnostic Gospels* on "God the Father / God the Mother," and in her *Signs* essay, "What Became of God the Mother?," this suppression amounted to a censorship of the gnostic portrayal of Christianity as far more feminine than the sanctioned texts of the New Testament even begin to indicate. As a result, there are tremendous gaps in the account of early Christianity that we have been given by select men who controlled its language and texts.

What is missing, for instance, is what Pagels calls "an extra-ordinary poem" from a text entitled *Thunder, Perfect Mind* spoken in a feminine divine voice:

> For I am the First and the last.
> I am the honored one and the scorned one.

> I am the whore and the holy one.
> I am the wife and the virgin. . . .
> I am the barren one,
> and many are her sons. . . .
> I am the silence that is incomprehensible . . .
> I am the utterance of my name. (xvi)

What is also missing is the *Gospel of Mary* that records Mary Magdalene's challenge to Peter in his role as institutional authority figure.
What is missing is the characterization of a divine mother as Wisdom,
indicating the feminine and procreative powers of knowledge.
According to some gnostics, she is responsible for teaching Adam and
Eve self-awareness, for guiding them to food, and assisting in the
conception of some of their children (64–65). Also missing are portrayals
of a male god jealous of his mother.

Many gnostic texts record various stories of the mother of the
presumed originary male god of Judeo-Christian traditions. Often
portrayed as Wisdom, she is variously distressed by her son and
castigates him for his presumption and jealousy. In one text, when the
male god exclaims that there is no one above him, his mother "'cried
out against him, "Do not lie, Ialdabaoth . . ."'" (69). According to
another text, when this male god exerts his exclusive power, we read
this story: "'And immediately Sophia ("Wisdom") stretched forth her
finger, and introduced light into matter, and she followed it down into
the region of Chaos. . . . And he again said to his offspring, "It is I who
am the God of All." And Life, the daughter of Wisdom, cried out; she
said to him, "You are wrong, Saklas!"'" (70). One gnostic text portrays
the feminine divine as a voice. Entitled the *Trimorphic Protennoia*,
meaning "Triple-formed Primal Thought," it reveals, according to
Pagels, "the feminine powers of Thought, Intelligence, and Foresight."
The text reads: "I am perception and knowledge, uttering a Voice by
means of Thought. [I] am the real Voice. I cry out in everyone, and they
know that a seed dwells within" (65–66).

This "Voice by means of Thought," intimately connected to a
conception of knowledge as palpable and seedlike, was emphatically
and promptly suppressed by church authorities. As Pagels points out in
her *Signs* essay, it would be a mistake to hastily assume that the gnostic
gospels "were suppressed only because of their positive attitude toward
women," yet as she explains, "the evidence does indicate that two very
different patterns of sexual attitude emerged in orthodox and gnostic
circles" (105). And, I would add, an oppositional dynamics of language.
In these gnostic stories, we hear multiple voices even as they are

contained in one voice ("I am the honored one and the scorned one"). We hear voices of disturbance and disagreement ("You are wrong, Saklas"). These are not controlling narratives, but stories filled with interference and response. To use de Certeau's terms, the voices here "enact" rather than confirm thought. In one gnostic text, for example, Peter complains to Christ that Mary Magdalene is dominating the conversation and, as Pagels explains, "displacing the rightful authority of Peter and his brother apostles. He urges Jesus to silence her and is quickly rebuked." Mary replies: "'Peter makes me hesitate; I am afraid of him because he hates the female race'" (78).

Now this is a story. In suppressing all of these voices that crowd and vex the gnostic gospels, those who established the literate canons of early Christianity in fact used literacy—as written word and as shared knowledge—to solidify only certain stories, and only certain kinds of stories. In the process, they suppressed not simply texts, but very specific "voices" and the distinctive ways of knowing that were connected to these voices, this language. As Pagels explains, the very meaning of *gnosis* is to know directly, to know through experience or insight: "*gnosis* is not primarily rational knowledge. The Greek language distinguishes between scientific or reflective knowledge ('He knows mathematics') and knowing through observation or experience ('He knows me'), which is *gnosis*" (xviii). The release of this kind of knowledge through Pagels's readings of the gnostic gospels marks a significant rupture in accepted literate traditions that have favored rational and scientific modes of knowing, just as it marks a rupture in the controlling authoritative voice of orthodox texts. While I do not want to strictly align these other voices and ways of knowing recorded in the gnostic gospels with oral traditions, I would suggest that their release works to unsettle the accepted canons of Christian literacy through volatile language and competing narratives—not the singular voice announcing the one meaning, but voices within that utter meanings, that continually utter thought itself. Stories upon stories unfold in Pagels's account of these gnostic texts, each interfering in different ways with the accepted narratives that orthodox Christian literate traditions have encoded. As Pagels tells us, she does not want to return the gnostic gospels to some position of originary authority, but "reopen" the story of early Christianity, to put more than one narrative in circulation, to reconsider and reinvent through the very process of telling and thinking through stories. I recall de Certeau: voice "alters a place (it disturbs), but it does not establish a place" (155).

Pagels herself engages such an altering critical narrative, a story that begins like a murder mystery but works toward no fixed conclusion or denouement—very much, as we will see, like the never-ending stories that fuel oral narrative. She begins her account of *The Gnostic Gospels* by relating how an Arab peasant, setting out to avenge his father's death, comes upon a buried urn containing thirteen papyrus books. Her story goes on to relate how these texts found their way onto the black market and were smuggled through various hands before some of them finally landed with scholars who recognized them as gnostic gospels. Yet this is not the end, but only the beginning of their story, which Pagels herself, among other scholars, has relied on for her particular critical narrative. As this narrative unfolds, different voices come to life—including the voice of Elaine Pagels as she retells stories about the shaping of early Christianity, a voice that has been crucial in the shaping of contemporary feminist criticism.

After reading Pagels once again, I turn back to Hirsch's *Cultural Literacy* and gloss the Appendix at the end, aptly entitled "What Literate Americans Know: A Preliminary List." As Hirsch explains, the list has been compiled by three professors at the University of Virginia, and is intended not to be limiting, but rather to "illustrate the character and range of the knowledge literate Americans tend to share" (146). I find, under the letter "G," reference to "Gospel," but not "gnostic gospels." And in their appropriate alphabetic slots, I find reference to the specific texts of "Matthew, Saint, Gospel according to," "Mark, Saint, Gospel according to," "Luke, Saint, Gospel according to," "John, Saint, Gospel according to." There is reference to "Jesus," and to "Mary, mother of Jesus," and, among the other references to the name Mary, including "Mary, Mary, Quite Contrary" and "Mary Had a Little Lamb," we also find "Mary Magdalene," though she is not designated as author of a gospel. There is mention of several other biblical texts, including "Job, The Book of," and simply "Ruth," followed by "Ruth, Babe," and "Genesis, The Book of," and "Ecclesiastes, The Book of," and "Paul, Saint," but not Deborah or Sarah or Rachael.

We could, of course, argue about what is included and excluded on this list of shared cultural knowledge. I will admit that I sometimes find myself worrying, with Hirsch, that many of the authors and texts that inform our rich cultural heritage are increasingly unknown to people educated in this country. But I worry more about their not knowing what is *not* on this list and what is likely to remain absent in any future lists. Even more, I worry that an insistence on standardized language will prevent us from understanding the function of language in shaping that knowledge, prevent us from hearing the shaping sounds of words. And here I do not mean only the mixed sounds of a multilingual culture, but the myriad hybrid qualities of language that inform empirical research, poetic expression, legal contract, dialogue, scientific theory, memoir, historical narrative, novel, religious testament.

For, as I will be suggesting throughout this book, the insinuation of sound and vocalization in writing can exert particular pressure on disciplinary language that keeps tightly controlled the very terms of its discourse and hence the knowledge it produces. Critical interferences here might make more fluid the firm and longstanding demarcation between what we classify as critical and literary writing—between the rhythms of poetry and rigors of abstraction and analysis, between objective stances and personal encounters, between narrative and philosophy, stories and science. How might legal theory sound like a story, and with what effects? How might science sound like a memoir, and why? What are the sounds of things, the tenor of words, that might interfere with critical messages?

Luce Irigaray, writing about women and language, begins her essay "When Our Lips Speak Together" with this caution: "If we keep on speaking the same language together, we're going to reproduce the same history. Begin the same old stories all over again. . . . The same discussion, the same arguments, the same scenes" (*This Sex* 205). Pagels hardly tells the same old story, but then what she uncovers is hardly the same old language. What shall we make of this voice that cries not singularly, alone from the wilderness, but cries out from various sites and voices within, voices that unpredictably and multiply move through a text? What shall we make of these heterogeneous vocal instigations within critical inscriptions?

2

Narrative Resonance

Stories abound in feminist theory, often excessively so. It is as if the voices telling these stories, or the voices emerging within them, simply cannot be contained within conventional narrative structure. Instead of predictable plots, we encounter unexpected twists and turns of thought; instead of neat conclusions, we have incommensurable messages. In this chapter, I want to ask what sound might have to do with these voices, what the oral dynamics of telling and retelling tales has to do with complex modes of knowing. Before engaging these questions, let me offer a couple of examples of these narratives.

The first is a story told by Judith Butler, when she herself will "risk an example" in order to "concretize" some questions about how post-modern positions can account for change. Her particular story unfolds at the Jewish Community Center where Butler swims. Here she encounters a water aerobics class in progress, composed of a "group of older Jewish women, most of them with very large thighs in a dancelike motion," who "were lifting their legs out of the water and splashing them down again to a remake of Tommy James and the Shondells' 'Mony, Mony.'" On looking closer, she sees that some of these women "had blue numbers on their arms from concentration camps—which," as she explains, "made me understand that these were compensatory thighs." As these women enter what Butler calls "the postmodern hybrid of 'hydrobics'" and the "'remake'" of an old song from "an adolescent culture they never had," she surmises that they are rein-venting themselves and their worlds. Watching them, and grasping the moment, Butler concludes: "I thought to myself that perhaps this was the collapse of temporal frames as the occasion for affirmation—and I dove in" ("Skeptical" 236).

My second example is from the opening chapter of Jane Flax's *Disputed Subjects*, in which she tells the story, traces the narrative, of her own theoretical writing. Although, as she says, it would be "pleasant" to relate a "straightforward" narrative, she describes instead how she feels "compelled to tell a more ambiguous story whose content mixes personal history and theoretical reflection" (3). As she traces the continual unfolding of her writing and thinking ("The longer I write, the more uncertain I become about any aspect of my theorizing") (7), Flax moves toward understanding her story about writing and theory as a kind of love story: "Throughout this narrative a theme recurs. A process similar to falling in love and then experiencing a certain amount of disillusionment pervades my intellectual history" (28–29). While this kind of disillusionment often leads to despair, as she explains in the unfolding of her story, postmodernism has proved for her to be "a particularly powerful antidote to political and philosophical despair" (30). The great Enlightenment narratives of truth and universal good turn out to be compelling yet flawed narratives that trace a straight-forward progression from ignorance to truth, darkness to light, con-fusion to certainty—as if this kind of progression ever really took us to a place of refuge. "As a child of the Holocaust," Flax explains in rejecting these narratives, "I cannot believe in a linear, progressive, or teleological view of history in which all suffering has a purpose and time only moves in one direction, toward the redemption of us all" (31). Like the women in the Jewish Community Center swimming pool, Flax negotiates her way in a world that is continually remaking itself, in narratives that continually reinvent reality.

Not only are Butler and Flax telling stories, thinking critically and theoretically through narrative, but the stories they relate do not follow a conventional plot that leads from beginning to end, conflict to resolution. In Butler's case, there are no particular beginnings and endings as she ponders the "collapse of temporal frames," but remakes of old songs that now take on different meaning, the continual recasting of lives. With Flax, narrative deliberately veers away from sequential plot. The story of her own engagement with postmodern theory will not settle with some denouement, but keep unfolding in an uncertain and always changing world in which we are ceaselessly engaged and accountable. Both critical narratives sustain linguistic and epistem-ological motion. Their meanings resonate.

And both stories—each haunted by the tragedy of the holocaust, yet each turning away from some historical or temporal narrative that proceeds from tragic conflict to resolution, from madness to reason—recast theory into a narrative that defies the stasis of conventional plot. In resisting and unsettling such orderly plots, they also resist the kinds of critical denouement associated with "master narratives" that trace a progression, as Jean-François Lyotard explains, from ignorance to knowledge, confusion to certainty, error to truth, darkness to light (xxiii–xxv). If, as Joan Scott suggests, we should read "for the 'literary'" in our search for meanings, then the literary narratives embedded in Flax and Butler's stories would resemble something more like the "polyvocal" and "dialogic" energies of narrative described by Bakhtin than Lyotard's description of progressive narrative sequence. Or more precisely, they would resemble the narrative strategies of women novelists that Rachael DuPlessis describes in her work *Writing Beyond the Ending*. For their stories resonate beyond expected resolutions; their narratives move like soundwaves, like bodies moving in water, re-creating themselves.

The study of how narrative sequence imposes itself on nonliterary narratives—from philosophy to legal theory, from science to psycho-analysis to history—has consumed the attention of an assortment of scholars who devote themselves to studies of narrative and narratology. As one such critic, Wallace Martin, explains, "What may prove to be the most important development in narrative theory during the next few years" is its application to varied critical discourses such as "history, biography, autobiography, and psychoanalysis" (9), and, I might readily add, feminist theory. Indeed feminist critics themselves are no stranger to this narrative turn of events. Many engage in the writing of history, or psychoanalysis, or even science, as if they were writing stories that follow conventional plots: stories of good or bad mothers, plots of sisterly love or vampirish stealth, revised feminist histories that correct flawed patriarchal accounts. Myriad driving narrative structures shape critical thought—in feminism and elsewhere.

But what I find more intriguing, and much more compelling, in feminist theory are those stories that veer away from conventional narrative structure, where theorists consciously work within narrative framework, but in the process rework the possibilities of narrative—collapsing its temporal frames and circling within an uncertain and unpredictable world that keeps exceeding denouement and conclusion. These writers not only insert narrative into theory, but transform both narrative and theory in the process. In terms used by narrative theorists, they rework what Hayden White calls the urge to represent events and ideas so that they "display the formal coherency of a story" that culminates in a desired "demand for closure" and a certain "moral meaning" (4, 21). Instead of settling with such coherency, these feminist critical narratives move in other directions. Their search for meanings is just as compelling as those that drive more conventional narrative, but they are imbued all the while with a kind of Bakhtinian "heteroglossia" and "polyvocality," welcoming what Christine Brooke-Rose calls the "glimmerings" of ideas and forms that are "protean, capturable for brief moments in language, but already changed even into their opposites another brief moment later" (Preface).

To return to my earlier question: What might such protean narrative have to do with sound, and with the particular kinds of kinetic meanings that emerge from the motion of words? To explain this connection, let me recall Michel de Certeau, whose ideas about residual traces of orality and "voices" within what he calls a "scriptural economy" I have explored in chapter 1. Let me turn now to his essay "Story Time," where he links orality and voice with the forces of narrative, and specifically associates narrative with the "art of speaking" (77). He explains that while "description" can represent and render "objects," narrative "produces effects" (79). In narrative, readers do not respond as if from a distance to some rendition of reality or ideas; rather, they actually engage the process of its production—its narrative utterance, its act of being spoken. And this process, in turn, recasts thinking itself, connecting thought to the effects of speech and voice. Citing, among others, Jack Goody's work on oral narrative tradition, de Certeau describes how the actual "practice" of narrative involves us in a dynamic engagement in thinking: "The storyteller falls in step with the lively pace of his fables. He follows them in all their turns and detours, thus *exercising* an art of thinking" (81, italics mine). "Story Time" is therefore a kind of narrative realm into which we can enter and actually participate—via speech and telling and listening and retelling—in a dynamic, "rambling" process of thought, what de Certeau calls, borrowing a term from Frontisi, "'labyrinthine intelligence'" (89–90). As de Certeau's examples from the narratives of history and anthropology show, this critical practice hinges on the connection of speech and thought, an "art of speaking which is an art of thinking and of operating" (79).

It is exactly this conjunctive operation of utterance and intelligence that I find permeating the self-conscious engagement with narrative among certain feminist critics and theorists. And it captures what I mean by narrative resonance—a dynamic, sometimes rambling, often intensely polyvocal engagement with stories that carry critical thought. Turning away from coherent narratives that lead, often fairly directly, from conflict to resolution, the feminist theorists I write about here use narrative to enter into a "story time" that unsettles easy resolutions and involves us instead in a complicated, labyrinthine practice of critical ruminations. This practice is instigated through the narrative dynamics of speech seized in writing, and as vocality permeates writing, writing itself is transformed.

We can follow this operation as it unfolds in diverse feminist critical contexts. Trinh Minh-ha, for instance, challenges distinctions between oral narrative as fictive and written philosophy as true: "For 'oral' and 'written' or 'written' versus 'oral' are notions that have been as heavily invested as the notions of 'true' and 'false' have always been" (*Woman* 126). Narrative thus continually establishes and moves beyond the confines of any static sense of truth. Trinh's own writing, as we will see, unfolds as both story and theory, a place where truth and narrative intermingle in the endless telling of stories. Nancy K. Miller describes her own "version of autobiographical writing" as "narrative criticism," and her book *Getting Personal* is filled with stories about the situations, contexts, and development of her own critical ideas. Yet far from reaching conclusions, Miller often ends with questions, ponderings. She brings one chapter to a tentative conclusion before adding a "coda," with the phrase "I will end here for now" (139). Gloria Anzaldúa describes the anthology *Making Face, Making Soul: Haciendo Caras* as an attempt to "teach ourselves and whites to read in non-white narrative traditions—traditions which, in the very act of writing, we try to recoup and to invent." In similar contexts, Barbara Christian insists that "people of color have always theorized—but in forms quite different from the Western form of abstract logic. And I am inclined to say that our theorizing . . . is often in narrative forms, in the stories we create, in riddles and proverbs, in the play with language, since dynamic rather than fixed ideas seem more to our liking" (336).

Donna Haraway emphasizes this same dynamic potential in narratives of science, and claims that feminist science does not correct flawed masculine narrative but engages the very narrative process of "changing possibilities." She describes her own essay "Primatology Is Politics by Other Means" as one which "works as a story . . . by a layering of meanings and deliberate punning; the attempt is to provide a convincing account of the history of science that is simultaneously political theory, science fiction, and sound scholarship" (81–82). More recently Madelon Sprengnether, in her essay "Ghost Writing: A Meditation on Literary Criticism as Narrative," engages her own practice of autobiographical criticism to explain how the writing of criticism always involves "creating a narrative." Pondering the development of her critical writing, Sprengnether notices how she is attracted to stories that somehow overlap with her own desires and experiences, and how she writes criticism as a way of engaging those very stories, making them part of hers, and hers part of them. Criticism becomes not some distanced and controlled statement about literary texts, but itself an engagement *in* fiction—"a refracted form of autobiography" (94). And it is continually reshaped by yet another dynamic force, what Sprengnether calls "the 'ghost' in narrative, the way in which writing is haunted by the unconscious" (93–94, 87).

I am reminded of de Certeau's claim that "narrativity haunts such discourse" as it "insinuates itself" into seeming objective, descriptive, analytic, and theoretical work (78). Each of the feminist critics I have just cited strikes me as remarkably aware of this process of insinuation. Each embraces the ghost, as it were, as a writing partner, an all too conspicuous player in the shaping of critical narratives. In the process, story and theory, narrative and thought, overlap. Thus Haraway calls her own critical writing "simultaneously political theory, science fiction, and sound scholarship." Sprengnether describes her critical essay as "an example of autobiographical writing and a form of storytelling, my point being that the practice of literary criticism participates in both these forms: fiction and autobiography" (87). Anzaldúa, refusing a demarcation between the "artistic" and the "functional," relates a narrative of her own narrative writing: "Nudge a Mexican and she or he will break out with a story. So, huddling under the covers, I made up stories for my sister night after night. . . . It must have been then that I decided to put stories on paper" (Borderlands 65).

I emphasize these distinctive narrative qualities of feminist criticism and theory because they show how feminist scholars proceed with an awareness of how certain dominant narratives, those inscribed in longstanding critical traditions, have limited the possibilities of both language and thought. In reworking narrative from within, they turn the ground that has supported the unacknowledged stories and plot lines of what we might call the master narratives of intellectual discourses. In this sense, the feminist turn toward engaging narrative in theory has become a vehicle for reworking our way through complex systems of discourse and power, thus clearing a space for what Haraway calls other "narrative possibilities" (Simians 3). As she explains with reference to her own study of primatology, "I am arguing that the struggle to construct good stories is a major part of the craft. There would be no primatology without skillful, collectively contested stories. And, there would be no stories, no questions, without the complex webs of power, including the tortured realities of race, sex, and class— and including people's struggles to tell each other how we might live with each other" ("Primatology Is Politics" 80).

Stories thereby become the critical site of change, and the changing site of criticism. Through them, we might "tell each other" our versions of the world—fictive and theoretical—and so engage a labyrinthine intelligence. Feminist theory becomes the story of that volatile, speaking intelligence.

This kind of speaking intelligence—thought that is continually reiterated and re-formed through dialogic narrative—has a long background in oral narrative traditions. While it would be a mistake to equate the varied narratives that sustain thought in oral cultures with contemporary critical narratives that engage what de Certeau calls "the art of speaking," we should not overlook the important connections that link these modes of narrative. Consider, for example, Berkeley Peabody's *The Winged Word*, a study of culturally diverse oral composition, showing how linear plot is incompatible with oral narrative which unfolds according to the storyteller's memory and interaction with specific listeners. Indeed one of the most distinctive qualities of oral narrative is its tendency to enact the immediacy and tumult of experience. A storyteller may well get carried away with a detail or delve into a flashback. Instead of following the kind of sequential structure of the typical climactic plot, oral storytellers are often driven by the episodic and ever-changing dynamics of life as it unfolds from day to day. Paula Gunn Allen suggests that such dynamics were at work in a particular Keres narrative before it was translated from its oral mode into western conflict-resolution structure. In her essay "Kochinnenako in Academe," Allen explains how "American Indian stories work dynamically among clusters of loosely interconnected circles," and in the case of this Keres narrative, most certainly do not follow the progression of a male hero from conflict to resolution (241).

Thus Walter Ong describes the structures of oral narrative as "episodic" rather than linear: "What made a good epic poet was not mastery of a climactic linear plot," but was, "among other things of course, first, tacit acceptance of the fact that episodic structure was the only way and the totally natural way of imagining and handling lengthy narrative, and, second, possession of supreme skill in managing flashbacks and other episodic techniques." As Ong observes, the classical notion of beginning an epic *in media res* is actually a literate structure modeled on the more or less haphazard ways in which oral narrators begin their stories (144). Oral stories can begin and end anywhere. They lack the kinds of linear temporal frames that structure written narrative. In saying this, however, we need to keep in mind the distinction between the *dynamics* and possible *effects* of oral narrative. For all its volatile unfolding, oral stories can be and certainly have been highly systematizing, serving as agents to enforce rigid, and often strikingly patriarchal, norms. Yet these same narrative dynamics may prompt very different scenarios, and work more like Bakhtin's "dialogic" forces in the novel, which unsettle the unifying, cohesive tendencies of language. I read feminist critical narratives as resonating in exactly this way, as sustaining sound and motion that permeate—like vibrations—the solid terrain of well-plotted ideas.

Such was the case when, earlier this century, Virginia Woolf pondered the sentences of a woman novelist who was "tampering with the expected sequence," not only with the sentences but a whole set of narrative expectations. Woolf describes how she turned the pages of a book and read the words "'Chloe liked Olivia.'" With these simple words, the entire heterosexual plot dissolved. "And then it struck me," Woolf explains, "how immense a change was there. Chloe liked Olivia perhaps for the first time in literature. Cleopatra did not like Octavia. And how completely *Antony and Cleopatra* would have been altered had she done so!" (85–86). Such disruptions of sentences and expected sequences can open for us what Haraway calls other "narrative possibilities," such as that recently uncovered by Carolyn Woodward in her discovery of a fascinating eighteenth-century narrative, *The Travels and Adventures of Mademoiselle de Richelieu*, a story of two women and lesbian desire. The effects of this desire, as Woodward shows, completely break with conventional narrative structure: "Linear expectations of plot are deferred or thwarted. Fragments are common, seeming digressions become central, and the ending hints at but finally refuses closure: contentment is both a state and a process, 'home' is mobile, and the joyful couple is neither married nor not married" (839).

I am certainly interested in such disruptive narrative, but I find myself even more interested in Woodward's own critical writing, which draws us into the narrative process of thought. For she, too, tells a story, a critical narrative, and implicates us in the very unfolding of this narrative. "It was summer, and rain splattered on the high windows of the British Library's north reading room. *Mademoiselle de Richelieu* arrived: three tiny volumes, crumbling leather covers tied up with muslin ribbons. I opened volume one, trying not to sneeze from the dust. A thin ray of sun shone aslant my page from one window, as I began to read about women's rights: the right to write, to travel alone, to cross-dress. Pages were brittle and cracking and sometimes falling from the bindings. I read on: the right to choose not to marry, to choose not to bear children" (838). As Jane Tompkins says when she finally gets hold of a piece of critical writing that grabs her attention (and especially for me as a critic who began my own research in the dusty files of eighteenth-century studies where never a word was uttered about lesbian narratives or poems): "I am completely hooked" (133). Or as de Certeau would have it, the narrative draws me in; I am now a part of its process and practice. Yet Woodward's essay does not only engage me through the story it tells, but also by drawing me into a novel that itself breaks with the kinds of conventional narrative structure that we were taught accounted for the infamous "rise of the novel." What we have is a critical narrative that reworks accepted critical structure, and a novelistic narrative that reworks typical fictional structure.

I find these kinds of destabilizing narratives emerging throughout feminist criticism and theory, questioning many of the longstanding assumptions that govern a variety of master narratives in diverse disciplines, indeed within feminism itself. Of course such critical narratives are hardly peculiar to feminists; yet to overlook their prevalence and intensity in feminist theory would be to miss one of its most distinctive and potentially transformative qualities. I would go so far as to suggest that the feminist self-conscious engagement with narrative marks a unique site on the contemporary scene of criticism and theory: for it unsettles some of the very narrative assumptions on which feminist thought has been built, yet in so doing, it mobilizes stories that keep feminist ideas lively and contentious.

For the remainder of this chapter, I want to delve into three particular works of feminist theory, each of which unfolds very self-consciously as a narrative, and in the process unsettles three dominant critical plots: colonial conquest, the history of science, and legal theory. These stories hardly signal a return to narrative coherence by replacing faulty critical narratives with new improved versions. Instead, their authors dive in, as Judith Butler did at the Jewish Community Center, to words and worlds that move, where narrative lets us reinvent and retell our lives, break the sequence of sentence and plot.

(6)

A story told is a story bound to circulate.

—Trinh, *Woman* (134)

When Trinh Minh-ha begins her book *Woman, Native, Other: Writing Postcoloniality and Feminism,* she tells a story about how people tell stories in a particular "remote village" where they have come together "to discuss certain matters of capital importance to the well-being of their community." Here she describes how the narrative unfolds:

Never does one open the discussion by coming right to the heart of the matter. For the heart of the matter is always somewhere else than where it is supposed to be. To allow it to emerge, people approach it indirectly by postponing until it matures, by letting it come when it is ready to come. There is no catching, no pushing, no directing, no breaking through, no need for a linear progression which gives the comforting illusion that one knows where one goes. (1)

In this book devoted to third-world women and writing—a narrative itself interspersed with still shots from Trinh's films, a book in which Trinh everywhere questions the static language of western writing and thinking—the subject of narrative becomes crucial. For as she says in the title of her opening section, "The Story Began Long Ago . . . ," long before "the immemorial days when a group of mighty men attributed to itself a central, dominating position vis-à-vis other groups . . ." (1). Trinh's own writing does not follow these centralizing perspectives, but moves as a narrative and into a narrative without beginning or end, one that continually flows like the oral exchanges and stories told by these people who have gathered for their meeting. Listening to Trinh's description of their stories, we might well get the impression that we have entered into a postmodern world without borders and boundaries, or into some scene from an avant-garde drama. In fact, we are listening to a group of oral people whose narratives and ways of thinking do not follow the dictates of strict linear progression.

Entering into this narrative and at the same time writing about it as a third-world woman who has emphatically crossed into western literacy, Trinh explains:

The story never stops beginning or ending. It appears headless and bottomless for it is built on differences. Its (in)finitude subverts every notion of completeness and its frame remains a non-totalizable one. The differences it brings about are not only differences in structure, in the play of structures and of surfaces, but also in timbre and in silence. We—you and me, she and he, we and they—we differ in the content of the words, in choice and mixing of utterances, the ethos, the tones, the paces, the cuts, the pauses. The story circulates like a gift; an empty gift which anybody can lay claim to by filling it to taste, yet can never truly possess. A gift built on multiplicity. One that stays inexhaustible within its own limits. (2)

The inexhaustible potential of language both fuels and becomes the subject of Trinh's writing. And such potential itself unfolds as an inexhaustible narrative. This is not some message that she delivers as a theorist of deconstruction (though such theory informs her writing). It is a message that she reiterates throughout her engagement with and as the person "who 'happens to be' a (non-white) Third World member, a woman, and a writer," who "often finds herself at odds with language, which partakes in the white-male-is-norm ideology and is used predominantly as a vehicle to circulate established power relations" (6). To break with such ideologies and power relations necessarily entails breaking with and refusing to write within the confines of a language that follows the plot lines of these scenarios. Trinh—as a writer, critic, theorist, and also as one not strictly identified by any of these labels— engages different narratives: stories without a beginning and end, stories of multiplicity. Enacting what some might describe as a postcolonial process that resists the centralizing forces of the oppressor and yet also refuses the idea of some original precolonial or "primitive" identity in neat opposition to the oppressor, Trinh writes in a hybrid and mixed world, and through language that releases the rich possibilities of meaning rather than working toward static definitions, easy conclusions.

And this inevitably, always, entails the incessant telling of stories that break with controlling master narratives. Scenarios continually unfold, in sometimes predictable and sometimes unimaginable ways. Trinh begins her book in the midst of "A Story That Began Long Ago," and moves toward a final chapter entitled "Grandma's Story" about the continually unfolding powers of narrative. Just as beginnings and endings exceed their fixed places in the plot, so do the very narrative voices that shape the telling of this critical narrative. Trinh wants to make more fluid the demarcations between critical and literary voice, between herself as a narrator in this book and two "literary" authors she writes about, Maxine Hong Kingston and Leslie Marmon Silko. As she explains in a different essay in *When the Moon Waxes Red*, "Theory is not necessarily art, and art not quite theory. But both can constitute 'artistically' critical practices whose function is to upset rooted ideologies, invalidating the established canon of artistic works and modifying the borderlines between theoretical and non-theoretical work" (226).

When Trinh writes narrative, and writes about narrative, in "Grandma's Story," she not only questions strict boundaries between critic and artist, but also between the kinds of literate, linear narrative told by critics and the more mobile and expansive narratives allowed in literature. Thus what she calls "the search for a unifying principle" that traditionally characterizes criticism gives way, through these permeable boundaries, to a "mutual counteraction" between criticism and art, where "critical practice is to shuttle incessantly between borders, with no one border having fixed priority over the others" (*Moon* 225–26). In many ways, I also see this kind of critical practice as a shuttle between the oral and the literate, where Trinh *writes* this process of shuttling back and forth, crossing the divides between critical "unifying" narratives and the "inexhaustible" language that feeds her writing. When she describes oral narrative, she is also describing her own movement between criticism and art, thinking and speaking:

> Storytelling, the oldest form of building historical consciousness in community, constitutes a rich oral legacy, whose values have regained all importance recently, especially in the contexts of writings by women of color. She who works at un-learning the dominant language of "civilized" missionaries also has to learn how to un-write and write anew. (*Woman* 148)

In one sense, the generation of different stories develops in opposition to western linear narrative, showing the limitations of its structure and possible scenarios. Yet what lies on the other side is not some better or more correct narrative, but narrative as unfolding possibilities—the episodic and multiplicitious dynamics characteristic of oral legacy and dialogic thought. Trinh sets up the opposition of the two modes before elaborating on the possibilities of breaking loose of this opposition. She cites a "man of the West" who claims that a good story "'must have a beginning that rouses interest, a succession of events that is orderly and complete, a climax that forms the story's point, and an end that leaves the mind at rest.'" To this she responds: "Life is not a (Western) drama of four or five acts. Sometimes it just drifts along; it may go on year after year without development, without climax, without definite beginnings or endings. Or it may accumulate climax upon climax, and if one chooses to mark it with beginnings and endings, then everything has a beginning and an ending" (142–43).

The possibilities generated by this opening of narrative structure reside in the very ongoing process of story telling. It is not that narrative must now be redirected so that it enforces certain other ideologies or political or cultural agendas. It is not that oral narrative will inevitably dictate certain plots and themes more congenial, say, to feminists or postcolonial theorists or whoever may want to set up a new narrative agenda. We are not left with agendas, but with the possibilities of reinvention. Trinh describes these possibilities as those kept alive by Leslie Silko's "Storyteller" who "keeps the reader puzzling over the story as it draws to a close. Again, truth does not make sense. It exceeds measure: the woman storyteller sees her vouching for it as a defiance of a whole system of white man's lies." In this system, we are given only certain narrative paths to follow, certain subscribed ways of writing and thinking. But "what is more important," Trinh says, "is to (re-)tell the story as she thinks it should be told; in other words, to maintain the difference that she allows (her) truth to live on. The difference" (150).

Seizing the dynamics of oral narrative may generate just that—the difference that will always allow for different stories to be told. The problem is that conventional plot lines often impede this process, which is why, I suspect, so many feminist writers—shuttling through and between criticism and literature, theory and art—are seeking other kinds of narratives. When Trinh, for example, brings her own critical book to an end, she retells "A Bedtime Story" by Mitsuye Yamada in which her father relates the story of an old woman seeking a place to sleep for the night. Dissatisfied with the conclusion of the story, the young listener turns to her father and shouts: "'That's the END?'" (*Woman* 151). With this question, we have the last words of both the bedtime story and Trinh's book. Both narratives are left open, both must be read and reread, pondered, puzzled over, and continually changed in the process. Both critical and narrative plots must be available for retelling and reinvention.

Few tell this story more powerfully than Maxine Hong Kingston, a recognized "novelist" whose books have nonetheless won awards for "non-fiction prose," an author who shuttles back and forth between fact and fiction, reality and story. In her essay "The Novel's Next Step," Kingston wonders how can we break loose from, get out of, dominant plot lines when the very novel itself is caught up in conflict and death, its readers "addicted to excitement and crisis" and worshiping "tragedy as the highest art." She tells us: "The dream of the great American novel is past. We need to write the Global novel" (39). For Kingston, this global novel would invent ways to survive in a world marred everywhere by destruction, invent ways to sustain connections through all sorts of mixings and matings, create livable scenarios for our damaged lives. She urges us to start the process, and, as she says, "maybe hurry creation, which is about two steps ahead of destruction" (37). For her part in this project, Kingston sketches the plot of her novel *Tripmaster Monkey*, the story of Wittman Ah-Sing and Taña De Weese who set about changing themselves and their world. And she ends her essay by beginning to sketch another story: "Once upon a time, China had three Books of Peace. Those books were hidden and never found, or they were burned, their writers killed, their reciters' tongues cut out. But we can retrieve the Books of Peace by envisioning what could be in them . . . " (41). Her process is fueled by retrieval and creation, memory and invention—the forces that drive the continual unfolding of narratives and the stories we keep telling each other.

For Trinh, Kingston's powers as a storyteller are to be seized exactly in this space where we can retell stories: "Tell it to the world. To preserve is to pass on, not to keep for oneself. A story told is a story bound to circulate" (*Woman* 134). Thus the story of "No Name Woman" in Kingston's novel *The Woman Warrior* can be "broken open," as Trinh would say, just as the story Kingston begins to tell about the Chinese "Books of Peace" can be set loose, reinvented through narrative. Trinh says of Kingston: "This, I feel, is the most 'truthful' aspect of her work, the very power of her storytelling" (135).

These and other powers of storytelling fuel Trinh's writing as she shuttles between truth and fiction, criticism and "creative" writing (not to mention her filmmaking). As a woman from the third world, her work might too easily be contextualized within oral traditions that continue to thrive throughout many nonwestern cultures, traditions that no doubt influence her writings. And yet Trinh is a writer acutely aware of those centralizing linguistic forces that restrict the imaginative and distinctly narrative possibilities of writing. As she explains in an essay from *When the Moon Waxes Red*, "Truth, however, is not attained here through logocentric certainties (deriving from the tendency to identify human telos with rationality)." In their dynamic ability to break with accepted plot lines, just as her own postcolonial writing breaks with rationality and certainty, stories, she explains, can "open onto the fantastic world of the imagination . . ." (13). Her own story here is not purely oral, but hybrid, mixing logos and imagination. It is a message related by numerous feminist critics and theorists who have seized narrative as a cite for instigating change, for creation and reinvention. "What narrative possibilities might lie in monstrous linguistic figures for relations with 'nature' for ecofeminist work?" Donna Haraway wonders (*Simians* 3). What indeed might narrative have to do with the reinvention of nature and science, and how might science be part of Trinh's "fantastic world of the imagination" and its "rich oral legacy"?

ⓖ

. . . stories spread.

—Haraway, *Simians* (108)

Introducing her book *Primate Visions*, Donna Haraway describes the dominant vision of primatology that she will be questioning:

The history of primatology has been repeatedly told as a progressive clarification of sightings of monkeys, apes, and human beings . . . The story of correct vision of primate social form has the same plot: progress from misty sight, prone to invention, to sharp-eyed quantitative knowledge rooted in that kind of experience called, in English, experiment. . . . But these histories are stories about stories, narratives with a good ending; i.e., the facts put together, reality reconstructed scientifically. These are stories with a particular aesthetic, realism, and a particular politics, commitment to progress. (4)

Sound familiar? These same master narratives, tracing progress from origins to revelation, ignorance to truth, drive a wide variety of writings within critical traditions. Yet whether we call these writings science or primatology or philosophy or history, they remain, as Haraway says, "stories about stories, narratives with a good ending." Turning her attention not only to this "story of correct vision" in primatology, but also to the narratives of several prominent women primatologists, Haraway has her own story to tell, one in which she shows how the stories about primate behavior related by these particular women have worked to restructure "the whole field of possible stories" (303). In doing so, they have not given us the truth about apes, but different stories, opening up other "narrative possibilities" for science. Nor has Haraway given us the truth about primatology, but she has given us a compelling story about the construction of what counts as scientific truth.

How might this process of destabilizing some stories and generating others tap into the dynamics of oral narrative? Haraway has made clear that she does not buy into any "orientalist stereotypes of the 'oral primitive'" that would enforce simplistic distinctions between what she calls "oral and written cultures, primitive and civilized mentalities . . ." (*Simians* 175). Nor do I. When she describes, in her "Cyborg Manifesto" essay, how writing and literacy have special significance for women of color and all colonized people, she links their writing to what she calls "cyborg writing," writing that "must not be about the Fall, the imagination of a once-upon-a-time wholeness before language, before writing, before Man" (174–75). I agree. Writing some return to orality will not take us to a place of refuge, of innocence. "Cyborg writing," as Haraway explains, "is about the power to survive, not on the basis of original innocence, but on the basis of seizing the tools to mark the world that marked them as other" (175).

And yet seizing these tools is a narrative act, an act of writing fueled by stories that will "mark the world" through the very different telling of very different stories. Haraway puts it this way: "The tools are often stories, retold stories, versions that reverse and displace the hierarchical dualisms of naturalized identities. In retelling origin stories, cyborg authors subvert the central myths of origin of Western culture" (175). What Trinh calls the "rich oral legacy" of narrative bears striking resemblance to Haraway's cyborg writing, stories without beginnings and endings, stories that unsettle the linear dynamics of narrative built on a progression toward truth and resolution. As Haraway says, "We have all been colonized by those origin myths, with their longing for fulfillment in apocalypse" (175). To write another story we need to break with this scenario, as Trinh says that Leslie Silko does when she "keeps the reader puzzling over the story as it draws to a close" (*Woman* 150). Describing how such stories might rewrite the "literal technologies—technologies that write the world, biotechnology and microelectronics," Haraway claims: "Feminist cyborg stories have the task of recoding communication and intelligence to subvert command and control" (175).

This task of subverting command systems, especially the commanding and controlling master narratives of criticism and theory, requires tapping into narrative powers of reinvention and re-creation, the very powers that fuel the continual unfolding of oral and dialogic narrative. To say this is not to return to "orientalist stereotypes of the 'oral primitive,'" but to bring the powers of orality to a literacy built on such stereotypes. It means destabilizing the massive structures of master narratives encoded in critical traditions, or as Haraway says, "restructuring the whole field of possible stories." How this can happen in science, and in feminism, is the task that Haraway engages, the story that she tells. And she "tells" it with remarkable flair.

In *Primate Visions*, this story keeps us puzzling about origins and endings, authorial constraints, readers' expectations, and the fascinating mirrorlike relationship between human primates and the ape primates they observe. As Haraway puts it, "monkeys, apes, and human beings emerge in primatology inside elaborate narratives about origins, natures, and possibilities" (5). While primatology constitutes a particularly compelling narrative field because humans as primates enter into these narratives, scientific practice in general is, as she explains, "a kind of story-telling practice—a rule-governed, constrained, historically changing craft of narrating the history of nature" (4). Some of the stories told by scientists follow the structure of certain master narratives, such as one of David Barash's works in sociobiology which, Haraway shows, makes "unbridled use of the literary devices and thematic structure of Genesis and its commentators" (*Simians* 73). Others unfold according to varied narrative dynamics. For example, Haraway describes how a particular narrative told by primatologist Sarah Blaffer Hrdy unfolds as "a political history of troops dominated by male combat and female and male conflicting reproductive calculations" (*Simians* 100). Whatever the situation, "attention to narrative" becomes not a way of turning away from real science, but a crucial means to "understand a particular kind of scientific practice that remains intrinsically story-laden—as a condition of doing good science" (331).

What is distinctive about the women primatologists that Haraway studies is hardly that they break away from such narratives or somehow manage to tell the truthful story about primate behavior, but that they bring to primatology a variety of narrative options. In other words, they create narratives that alter the scientific field. The fact that large numbers of women have entered into primatology and that many of them have produced destabilizing narratives indicate that scientific stories are to a large extent shaped by matters of sex and gender, among a host of other influences such as "class, race and nation," and that the process of unsettling the dominant plots of science should therefore be of crucial interest to feminists. Haraway explains the connection in this way: "Feminism is, in part, a project for the reconstruction of public life and public meanings; feminism is therefore a search for new stories, and so for a language which names a new vision of possibilities and limits. That is, feminism, like science, is a myth, a contest for public knowledge" (*Simians* 82). It is not that "one story is as good as another," but that "comparative stories about people and animals" constitute a crucial means of understanding and reconstructing nature; they "set the historical conditions for imagining plots" (*Simians* 105–7). In this sense, Haraway's own critical writing is itself not a new feminist story, but as she puts it, a "tale of the transformation of stories . . ." (*Simians* 105).

As I have been trying to show all along, this kind of transformation of stories and theories—from Elaine Pagels's accounts of the gnostic gospels to Haraway's accounts of women primatologists—relies on the dynamics of narrative to resonate, to generate and regenerate stories that expand the possibilities of thinking and writing. Yet now that the narrative field has been opened, questions linger about all these contesting narratives. Which are we to believe, which to dismiss? How can we navigate our way through these unfolding stories in an effort to understand what particular insights may be variously compelling, biased, racist, comforting, outrageous, helplessly political, positively political? Here, too, I think an understanding of dynamic oral narrative can help us assess the kinds of continual interaction and response that shape and reshape narrative. When stories are told in oral cultures, they are not simply presented in some set or final version to a quiet audience. Far from that, narrators and audiences are continually interacting. Certain audience responses may encourage a story teller to change the direction of her story, others may cause her to emphasize certain characters and actions and deemphasize or eliminate others. In turn, storytellers rely on their listeners for cues that might send them delving into a flashback or jumping ahead to some new scenario. The whole narrative process is one of intense engagement and interaction.

A similar set of activities may be put to work as strategies in reading written narratives, as the whole field of reader-response criticism has shown. Despite claims that authorial intention or direction drive the message of a narrative, readers may well interrupt texts in a variety of ways—by reading against the grain (I think of Judith Fetterley's "resisting reader"), by reading deliberately to subvert norms (as with numerous "queerings" of ostensibly "straight" texts), by stipulating authorial intentions for anonymous texts (as if responding to Terry Eagleton's questions: Who wrote *Casablanca*? Who wrote the Bible?)—in short, by willfully adopting or casually engaging the written text as an opportunity for interaction. As Jonathin Boyarin points out, the volatile act of reading itself destabilizes oral/literate contrasts by reshaping the fixed written word into something very much like the fluid oral utterance (3–4).

When Haraway emphasizes the importance of producing a variety of contesting and comparative stories, I believe she advocates the very kinds of lively interaction that mark such fluid oral utterances. Master narratives that drive the plots of critical traditions (even within feminism) have tended to downplay such interactive energies, in part because, as Trinh observes, the western emphasis on "clear" and "correct" language drives writing toward the production of "*an unambiguous message*" (*Woman* 16)—that hallmark of science. But people, unlike such coherent messages, are different, and we will all tell different stories. The cost of such polyvocality may be confusion and chaos—the production of babble. But the gain can be an increased sensitivity to different utterances and positions—a thoughtful confluence of the vocal and audible.

Haraway describes this process in her essay "Reading Buchi Emecheta" as one which comes alive through contested and interactive readings. Here she works her way through three critical readings, critical narratives, of a story told by the Nigerian novelist Buchi Emecheta, in an effort to show how "readings exist in a field of resonating readings, in which each version adds tones and shapes to the others, in both cacophonous and consonant waves" (*Simians* 113).

Haraway's metaphors of sound are unmistakable: readings "resonate," stories have "tones" that are "cacophonous" and "consonant." Her point is that feminists cannot risk perpetuating a "closed narrative" for any of our stories, especially those, such as Emecheta's and her readers', which delve into the complexity of "women's experience" in a global postcolonial world. We are all different, and we have different stories to tell. And this telling, this utterance, resonates in wavelike motion through our writings and our readings. To reduce them all to one feminist narrative—that would govern novels or science—limits meaning as severely as the efforts of dominant thinkers and writers to reiterate only certain master narratives. Instead, by telling our specific stories, by allowing a multiplicity of stories to be told, we can articulate our specific historical and cultural positions and use them to negotiate both our differences and connections. Haraway explains: "Complexity, heterogeneity, specific positioning, and power-charged difference are not the same thing as liberal pluralism. . . . The politics of difference that feminists need to articulate must be rooted in a politics of experience that searches for specificity, heterogeneity, and connection *through struggle*, not through psychologistic, liberal appeals to each her own endless difference. . . . Experience, like difference, is about contradictory and necessary connection" (109). In her "Cyborg Manifesto" essay, she puts it this way: "This is a dream not of a common language, but of a powerful infidel heteroglossia" (181). Once again we return to voice, but not some single feminist voice—rather a textual world resonating with multiple voices, with the motion and meanings produced by sound.

Yet such heteroglossia has hardly been the distinguishing feature of critical narrative traditions that have worked to codify meaning rather than acknowledge multiple and changing meanings. One might well argue that the "demand for closure" and "moral meaning," as Hayden White describes this imperative in historical narrative (21), actually cuts off the possible effects of heteroglossia before we even have the chance to engage and adjudicate these meanings. In embracing narratives that keep changing and unfolding even as we write and read them, we can at least *inter*act, move between and among stories and positions and interpretations. Writing and reading might be propelled by the lively dynamics of storytelling that keeps us productively "puzzled," endlessly engaged, and continually in the process of making judgments, discerning values, reshaping thought. In the narratives of primatology, certain stories will emerge—through the interaction of observers, writers, and readers—that prove to be more compelling, somehow more truthful, than others, before these narratives themselves become contested in a dynamic interactive community of scientists and commentators. Thus when Haraway introduces her work *Primate Visions*, she writes: "I want this book to be responsible to primatologists, to historians of science, to cultural theorists, to the broad left, anti-racist, anti-colonial, and women's movements, to animals, and to lovers of serious stories" (3).

In narratives produced by those particular female primates known as feminists, certain narratives will also emerge that prove to be variously compelling, disturbing, sexist, boring, or tantalizing, before they too fold over into and become other narratives within an intensely engaged and interactive group of storytellers. For me, that is what drives feminist theory—the willingness to take on and engage narratives, to understand how they have been constructed and to participate in their ongoing reinvention. In her essay "Situated Knowledges," Haraway writes: "We need the power of modern critical theories of how meanings and bodies get made, not in order to deny meaning and bodies, but in order to live in meanings and bodies that have a chance for the future" (187). And that is why we need feminist critical and theoretical narratives, so that we have the chance to enter into stories that unfold within "complex webs of power" and "tortured realities." So that we can "tell each other how we might live with each other."

I think this is what Leslie Silko had in mind when she wrote:

> I will tell you something about stories
>
> . . .
>
> They are all we have, you see,
> all we have to fight off
> illness and death.
>
> You don't have anything
> if you don't have the stories.

It is not that we need to find the right story to survive; it's that we survive through the retelling of stories—in fiction, and in theory.

ⓖ

> How will they ever pass the bar with subway stories? I am called to the dean's office.
>
> —Williams, *Alchemy* (28)

Stories of tortured realities. Stories about how we might live with each other—in subways and in social contract. These stories unfold as legal theory in Patricia Williams's book *The Alchemy of Race and Rights*, a book that begins with Williams telling us how depressed she feels on a particular morning and ends with the rage of polar bears. Subtitled *Diary of a Law Professor*, the book is not easy to categorize, packed as it is with personal observations, narrative after narrative, and yes, substantial legal commentary. In a brief section entitled "A Word on Categories" almost hidden at the end of her book (between Notes and Acknowledgments and Index), Williams relates how librarians want to catalogue the book according to certain topic areas such as "Afro-Americans" and "Civil Rights," though she wants her editor to "hold out" for the categories of "Autobiography" and "Fiction." She explains:

> This battle seems appropriate enough, since for me the book is not exclusively about race or law but also about boundary. While being black has been the most powerful social attribution in my life, it is only one of a number of governing narratives or presiding fictions by which I am constantly reconfiguring myself in the world. Gender is another, along with ecology, pacifism, my peculiar brand of colloquial English, and Roxbury, Massachusetts. (256)

These "governing narratives" are hardly stories that she tells for entertainment. Nor do their plots take us down the road toward denouement and resolution. They are not stories strictly about race or gender or language or Massachusetts, because they cross the boundaries of all of these topics. They also cross, and in the process, blur the boundaries between studies that we might otherwise strictly demarcate as legal writing or fiction, race relations or autobiography. Or feminist theory.

"That life is complicated is a fact of great analytic importance," Williams writes. She proposes an analysis of this complexity through stories, especially those that question the "governing narratives" that go under the name of law and the sanction of truth. Her narrative mode of writing may well reflect what Williams calls her "peculiar brand of colloquial English"—that quality itself remarkably vocal; yet she adopts narrative very deliberately, for the specific purpose of challenging those formal modes of writing and thinking that have exclusively shaped legal studies and the law itself. Williams begins by relating a conversation with her sister. She relates how she is writing "a book on law and liberation," one in which she "'will attempt to apply so-called critical thought to legal studies'" and do so "'in a way that bridges the traditional gap between theory and praxis.'"

"'But what's the book *about?*' my sister asks, thumping her leg against the chair impatiently.

"'Howard Beach, polar bears, and food stamps,' I snap back. 'I am interested in the way in which legal language flattens and confines in absolutes the complexity of meaning inherent in any given problem; I am trying to challenge the usual limits of commercial discourse by using an intentionally double-voiced and relational, rather than traditionally legal black-letter, vocabulary'" (6–7).

Since I, too, am interested in the way that most forms of critical writing, including legal language and theory, confine the complexity of meaning, I am once again, as Jane Tompkins would say, "completely hooked." Here is a book that will not only challenge legal language, but do so by telling stories, by engaging narrative, as a way of rethinking the law. Talking to her sister about language, Williams describes her reaction to traditions of writing and the law:

"Legal writing presumes a methodology that is highly stylized, precedential, and based on deductive reasoning. Most scholarship in law is rather like the 'old math': static, stable, formal— rationalism walled against chaos. My writing is an intentional departure from that. I use a model of inductive empiricism . . . in order to enliven thought about complex social problems. . . . I hope that the gaps in my own writing will be self-consciously filled by the reader, as an act of forced mirroring of meaning-invention. To this end, I exploit all sorts of literary devices, including parody, parable, and poetry."

"'. . . as in polar bears?' my sister asks eagerly, alert now, ears pricked, nose quivering, hair bristling.

"'My, what big teeth you have!' I exclaim, just before the darkness closes over me" (7–8).

Now this is a story. And it is filled with many stories, as Williams says, that take her "into the deep rabbit hole of this book" (5). It is told in reaction and contradistinction to the "static, stable, formal" narratives of legal language. And it dives into the detailed, complex, and mirroring dynamics of oral narrative, where storytellers and readers interact, filling in the gaps, continually reinventing meaning. No surprise, then, that the details begin to emerge in the midst of a conversation, a notably oral exchange between interlocutors, the place where reaction and response feed the continual unfolding of this series of narratives.

When Williams defines what she calls the "three features of thought and rhetoric" that characterize "theoretical legal understanding," it is as if she were pointing exactly to those distinguishing features of critical narrative and its conventional plots. There is first the "hypostatization of exclusive categories and definitional polarities" as in "rights/needs, moral/immoral, public/private, white/black" that govern the way we think. These "bright lines," as Williams calls them, everywhere define the workings of the analytical mind as it carves up and demarcates whatever it studies, working toward what Trinh would call *"an unambiguous message."* And then, second, we have the "existence of transcendent, acontextual, universal legal truths or pure procedures." This "essentialized world view," as Williams describes it, works from and toward the kind of static facts and essences that Havelock, for one, associated with the rise of western philosophical thought and its connections with literacy. Not surprisingly, such language turns away from the situated, specific, contextual dimensions of oral language and narrative, or as Williams explains, it promotes "a worrisome tendency to disparage anything that is nontranscendent (temporal, historical), or contextual (socially constructed), or non-universal (specific) as 'emotional,' 'literary,' 'personal,' or just Not True." The third feature of legal theory that Williams challenges is also a hallmark of dominant critical narratives, and that is its assumption of the "existence of objective, 'unmediated' voices by which those transcendent, universal truths find their expression"—not just lawyers and judges, but any assortment of "real people" who have some fixed claim to truth, who will tell us the final story (8–9).

In more dialogic narrative, of course, there is no final story, but the continual unfolding of stories through which versions of truth and meaning are always in the process of formation, reconsideration, reinvention. Life is complicated. Barely a dozen pages into her book Williams begins to tell stories that reflect the complications of law and life. The first is about her teaching and a particular story she tells her students. Describing an event she witnessed on Fifth Avenue in New York, in which parents correct their child for being afraid of a big dog, Williams explains: "I used this story in my class because I think it illustrates a paradigm of thought by which children are taught not to see what they see; by which blacks are reassured that there is no real inequality in the world, just their own bad dreams; and by which women are taught not to experience what they experience, in deference to men's ways of knowing" (13). Yet her law students, perhaps already too well trained in literacy and its epistemological traditions, don't like the story. "My students, most of whom signed up expecting to experience that crisp, refreshing, clear-headed sensation that 'thinking like a lawyer' purportedly endows, are confused by this and all the stories I tell them in my class on Women and Notions of Property" (14). They complain to the dean. Williams, meanwhile, tells more stories to her students, "stories of the deep-rooted commonplaces of our economically rationalized notions of humanity" (27). After telling one about a homeless man who appeared to be dead on a subway bench, her students again "rush to the dean to complain. They are not learning real law, they say, and they want someone else to give them remedial classes. How will they ever pass the bar with subway stories?"

While her students rush to the dean, Williams is rushing across boundaries, moving back and forth between the universal codes of "crisp" legal language and the everyday situated experiences she relates through narrative. What's more, she is questioning certain established narrative plots through her deliberate telling of other stories. Her students and the dean want resolution, but Williams keeps going deeper into her stories, layering versions upon versions. For example, she tells the story of how she was denied entrance at a Benneton's store, apparently for no other reason than her "round brown face" (44). Attempting to deal with her rage, she goes home and writes about the event in her journal, then types the story on a poster and sticks it in the Benneton store window. "So that was the first telling of this story," Williams explains. "The second telling came a few months later, for a symposium on Excluded Voices sponsored by a law review." For this story, she writes an essay connecting her experience at Benneton's on the damaging effects of increased privatization, especially "in response to racial issues" (47). The editors deleted all mention of race. Williams continues, "That was the second telling of my story. The third telling came last April, when I was invited to participate in a law-school conference on Equality and Difference." Here she repeats her tale, this time focusing on law review editorial procedures that are "rooted in a social text of neutrality." This is followed by a fourth telling of the story, this time by the local newspaper who reported on her talk at the law-school conference. The reporter completely misunderstood and misrepresented her ideas. And so the story goes. The fifth version is, of course, here in her book. Yet Williams does not bring the narrative to some resolution. She ends her chapter on this particular story with a series of questions that she is often asked about the stories—and leaves them unanswered, lingering.

What do all of these stories, all of these questions, mean? We will have to fill in the gaps. As readers, we will have to enter into the stories, interact with Williams, become part of the interpretive and narrative process that keeps unfolding. We will have to resist the tendency of dominant narratives to rush us toward conclusion, the *"unambiguous meaning.*" Stories like these continually emerge throughout Williams's book, pulling us into its rabbit hole, forcing us to read and engage in narrative dynamics that variously relate and resist the word of the law. There are stories about Williams's experiences attending Harvard Law School, about the wording of certain law examinations, about Howard Beach, about the Rockettes, about "Eleanor Bumpers, a 270-pound, arthritic sixty-seven-year-old woman" who wielded a knife as she was being evicted from her apartment, and was shot to death by a police officer. And there are endless stories about television and the stories it tells. Life is complicated. Mrs. Bumpers, for instance, said that she saw Ronald Reagan coming through her walls. Williams relates and responds to these narratives: "All these words, from the commissioner, from the mayor, from the media and the public generally, have rumbled and resounded with the sounds of discourse; we want to believe that their symmetrical, pleasing structure adds up to discourse; and if we are not careful, we will hypnotize ourselves into believing that it is discourse. When the whole world gets to that point, I know that I, for one, will see Ronald Reagan, clear and sprightly, coming through my walls as Mrs. Bumpers alleged he did in her last hours. And I have not yet been able to settle within myself whether that would be the product of psychosis" (142–43).

Legal discourse sets out to be symmetrical and structured, but it turns out to be nothing more than the narrative codification of rumbling sounds disguised as coherent discourse. Williams confronts these sounds with her own narrative rumblings, multiplying meanings and thereby exposing the limitations of universal legal codes. Narrative dynamics afford one way of breaking through the symmetry and structure of such codes. And oral language may play a crucial role in this destabilization. Jack Goody, who has written extensively on oral-literate contrasts, documents in his book *The Logic of Writing and the Organization of Society* the myriad ways in which diverse oral cultures base morality on specific situations rather than universal codes, while the acquisition of literacy in those cultures tends to solidify morality into legal codes that apply across the board. His arguments bear some resemblance to those of Carol Gilligan, whose findings about the relational and situational qualities of women's moral decision-making are detailed in her study *In a Different Voice*—an influential and much debated text that helped establish, among other subjects, the metaphor of voice in feminist theory. In whatever ways that literacy and gender influence matters of morality and law, Williams herself clearly engages narrative as a way to break the stasis of established legal codes, to force a changing and mobile sense of the law. As she explains, "Cultural needs and ideals change with the momentum of time; the need to redefine our laws in keeping with the spirit of cultural flux is what keeps a society alive and humane" (139).

Even in the most inhumane of circumstances. The story that haunts all of Williams's narratives is the one she tells about discovering the "contract of sale" specifying the trade of her great-great-grandmother among slaveholders. From this document, she tries to piece together—through stories and imagination—what it was like to be her great-great-grandmother, and what it is like to be her descendant. Yet the pieces do not easily come together, miraculously forming some whole, some complete and finished story. Since the sale of her great-great-grandmother, the law has changed. Yet stories of that law, stories of people who inherit that law and live in its unfolding narrative, continue. Consider the stories about Tawana Brawley, a fifteen-year-old black girl who was found alive in a plastic garbage bag. She had been raped, her body brutally disfigured and horribly abused. Williams tells Tawana Brawley's story in detail, details that belong to her own account of this tragedy. But what I do want to recall here from her description is how it unfolds through narrative upon narrative, how Williams repeats and makes us relive those narratives, how in the process of telling these stories, legal codes fade in the background while the details about specific people and situations come to life. As Williams explains, many "versions" of the story circulate before Tawana Brawley is "finally able to tell her story," only to be "replaced" by "a thunderous amount of media brouhaha, public offerings of a thousand and one other stories, fables, legends, and myths" (170–71). In a mad "quest" to finally find out "'what happened,'" we have more and more stories, each with their own special claim to the truth.

I believe that Williams risks retelling this story, risks reengaging the whole sordid process, because she, like Haraway, though in very different contexts, wants to reach readers who take stories seriously—who know that we construct our lives according to the stories we tell, and that through the retelling of stories we can figure out, maybe, how to live with each other. There is no neat conclusion to the story of Tawana Brawley, or to the story of Williams's great-great-grandmother. In the midst of all the emerging narratives, Tawana Brawley remains silent, "her mouth is closed." In retelling the story, Williams cannot speak for this young girl, but she can do what the best storyteller does among those who take stories seriously. She can engage those spell-casting powers described by Trinh: "The storyteller has long been known as a personage of power. . . . But her powers do more than illuminate or refresh the mind. They extinguish as quickly as they set fire. They wound as easily as they soothe" (*Woman* 126). Williams can, and does, leave us with haunting images from all the stories told about Tawana Brawley—images and stories that we now have to work through, retell, make some sense of in a dangerous and dangerously ambiguous world.

A world populated with polar bears. Here is another set of stories that only Williams can tell—about real polar bears who go crazy at a zoo, polar bears who keep emerging in stories told by her godmother, polar bears who keep appearing in her dreams. The ferocity and peace of polar bears: "Freshly ruffled fur, gleaming with fish oil, sleek with sacrifice and fire, smelling of smoke and bone chips. Polished leather paws, clean-eared and long-whiskered. A different ethic, brought to me from a world beyond difference" (213). Following the appearances and movements of polar bears throughout *The Alchemy of Race and Rights* is one of the most powerful critical engagements with narrative that I have experienced, so much so that I am reluctant to retell it (even if I could) in my own summary fashion. Because, of course, it eludes summary; the stories keep reverberating. That may be the important message—that there is no single referent for polar bears in these narratives, that their meanings keep moving. In one account, Williams describes being terrified by visions of polar bears, which she connects with her own awareness of motion and voice:

> It is wise, in a way, for me to be constantly watching myself, to feel simultaneously more than one thing, and to hear a lot of voices in my head: in fact, it is not just intelligent but fashionable, feminist, and even postmodern. It is also wise, I know, to maintain some consciousness of where I am when I am other than the voice itself. If the other voice in my head is really me too, then it means that I have shifted positions, ever so slightly, and become a new being, a different one from her, over there. It gets confusing sometimes, so I leave markers of where I've been, particularly if it's not just a voice but a place that I want to come back to in time. This season, those spots are marked with polar bears. (207–8)

And then again, her entire narrative is marked with polar bears—creatures of tremendous matter and weight that nonetheless move us, make it possible to unsettle, turn, and shift positions, change, and return, and set out all over again.

These polar bears, continually described by Williams as listening to her from "beyond language," also powerfully mark those places in language where sound beckons. This narrative, after all, is about telling and listening. Confronting her vision of the bears, Williams writes of this haunting exchange:

> I speak to them of the law: The Law. . . . I notice suddenly that I am making no sense. I am babbling, though my words are heavy-jawed and consequential. My words are confined and undone; I am tangled in gleaming, bubbled words. I hear the sounds of my own voice but they make no sense. . . . I speak to the distance of emptiness, I speak in circles and signals, I speak myself into the still.
>
> I am seized with the golden-weighted, heavy-hearted fear. (208–9)

I have no critical narrative to offer that straightens out these tangles of sound and voice. But Williams's critical narrative draws me into them. This may be the promise of such stories—that we are "tangled" in their "gleaming, bubbled words."

In a "Postscript" to another account of polar bears, Williams relates how she sent much of this book chapter to a prominent law review. It was rejected, as she explains in her own "paraphrased composite of rejection after rejection after rejection," because it lacked a "'clear statement of what the issue is,'" it lacked "'any climaxing of emotion,'" it needed to be rewritten as "'objective commentary.'" She is being called on to make her writing into more coherent narrative—clearer and unambiguous, better organized, distanced from its subject. But there is another possibility. The rejection continues: "'or, since you have a poetic way of writing, you should consider writing short stories'" (214).

Of course that's exactly what Patricia Williams is writing. Short stories. Narrative. Critical theory. Legal studies. And as the sixth, and final, Library of Congress catalogue tag indicates on the copyright page of *The Alchemy of Race and Rights*, "Feminist criticism."

3

Resounding Bodies

Feminist reclamations of the female body—from the ravages of intellectual chauvinism, artistic representation, and sexual repression, to mention only a few of its consigned haunts—mark perhaps the most longstanding and long-debated subject of feminist theory.[1] Indeed the very question of how the body insinuates itself in feminist theoretical writing shapes a fascinating topic all its own. Pondering the implications of what she calls "the body in theory," Trinh Minh-ha has this to say: "But thought is as much a product of the eye, the finger, or the foot as it is of the brain" (*Woman* 39).

And what, I would ask, of the ear? Or the way sound—heard, felt, imagined—can carry meaning along the skin, through tissue and the live wires of nerves, rebounding through brain and body? How might thought be a product of sound, and how might sound stir up rhythms, vibrations, and meanings in critical writing?

I want, in this chapter, to indulge another feminist engagement with the body, but this time by listening for the ways in which bodies serve as conduits of sonorous language, and how such sounding language in turn serves as a conduit of theory. My main effort here will be to retrace some prominent feminist arguments about writing the body, especially as they have developed through French traditions of *l'ecriture feminine*, to show how these texts are themselves steeped in language of and about sound. I also mean this chapter to work as a sort of interlude, a way for us to pause and reconsider some founding feminist theories about the body as a crucial source of both sonorous and somatic modes of thinking that have subsequently influenced a wide range of feminist theory—from the vocal and oral dimensions of narrative that I earlier explored, to theories about tactile, erotic, and poetic thought that I will be turning to in my final chapters. For despite the numerous feminist critiques of specular, visual economies, I believe we still need to understand how these critiques are indebted to an understanding of heard language, language that evokes messages beyond what we see symbolically represented on the page.

I turn to the body, then, as a conduit of sound, an oral conduit for theory. I want to pay special attention to the sounds of words which, in their very utterance, even in our quiet mouthing of them, echo the audible sensations of vowels, consonants, diphthongs—the stretched "o" of "longing," the crisp "c" of "critique." To speak of these sound-ings and mouthings of words brings us back to the whole matter of voice, for as Kaja Silverman says, the "voice is the site of perhaps the most radical of all subjective divisions—the division between meaning and materiality." She quotes Denis Vasse's claim that voice is situated "'in the partition of the organic and organization, in the partition between the biological body and the body of language, or, if one prefers, the social body'" (44). In this sense, to pay attention to voice is necessarily to pay attention to the body—biologically, linguistically, even culturally. But even more important to my argument, I want to inquire into how an attention to the sounding voice affects meaning, how sound keeps language moving with the body, and how this kinesis sustains a crucial destabilization of thought. Just as the feminist engagement in narrative, as I discussed in the previous chapter, works to keep generating narrative possibilities rather than confirm some correct story, so I would suggest that the feminist engagement with bodies in writing works to sustain the effects of sound, meanings that resound beyond definitions and final determinations. The very sonorous workings of language force us to listen, negotiate, adjudicate critical suggestions and speculations. Theory becomes less a matter of seeing clearly from a given perspective, and more a continual effort to respond to messages heard in the overt and covert suggestibility of words.

In saying this, I would further submit that feminist theory will not be invoked or remembered for any single statement that it proposes, but for multiple articulations that it sets loose. In this way, it acts more like a catalyst, like a body stirring up language and thought, and less like a voice crying from the wilderness, uttering a single message. To a large extent, this means that feminist theory unfolds more like a poem, an idea that I develop in my final chapter, proffering multiple signi-fications and interpretations, and less like the sorts of facts and statements that have tended to characterize critical expression. Trinh describes this poetic cast when she writes about the body in theory: "Instances where poeticalness is not primarily an aesthetic response, nor literariness merely a question of pure verbalism. And instances where the borderline between theoretical and non-theoretical writings is blurred and questioned, so that theory and poetry necessarily mesh, both determined by an awareness of the sign and the destabilization of the meaning and writing subject. To be lost, to encounter impasse, to fall, and to desire both fall and impasse—isn't this what happens to the body in theory?" (*Woman* 42).

Trinh is hardly the only feminist theorist who makes claims for destabilization and impasse, rather than clarity and coherence, as productive catalysts of critical thought. I'm reminded as well of Susan Griffin: "I love that moment in writing when I know that language falls short. There is something more there. A larger body. Even by the failure of words I begin to detect its dimensions. As I work the prose, shift the verbs, look for new adjectives, a different rhythm, syntax, something new begins to come to the surface" (8). For Griffin, words succeed through their very failure to stay still, their ability to suggest more than what it said, to shift, to respond to different rhythms. These are all effects of sound, and for Griffin, they are also effects intimately connected to the body, and particularly to her critique of a "transcendent, disembodied mind" serving as the "central trope of our intellectual heritage" (3).

I believe we need to understand how the infamous mind/body split is implicated in the deprecation and repression of sound in writing—not only in critical writing, to be sure, but emphatically in critical writing where aspirations to intellectual stasis and an unquestioning quietude pervade discourse. Hélène Cixous, whose call to women to write the body appeared nearly fifteen years ago in her resounding essay "The Laugh of the Medusa," knows all too well about the prevailing devaluation of sound in writing. In an interview, she explains her own preference for the "phonic and oral dimensions of language" over the "banal, clichéd language" where "one is far removed from oral language." Explaining how she tries "to write on the side of a language as musical as possible," she turns to the body as resource:

> I think that many people speak a language that has no rapport with the body. Instead of letting emerge from their body something that is carried by voice, by rhythm, and that would be truly inspired, they are before language as before an electric panel. They chose the hypercoded, where nothing traverses. But I think, and everybody knows, that there are other possibilities of language, that are precisely *languages*. That is why I always privilege the ear over the eye. I am always trying to write with my eyes closed ("Exchange" 146–47).

So much has been written on Cixous's volatile essay that I hesitate to return to what many feminists no doubt consider well-worn territory. But I believe that her preference for oral, sounding language that she discusses in this interview can help us understand why Cixous is anything but the essentialist she is so often accused of being. Her call is not for a mode of writing that will correspond to some static conception of woman's body, but far from that, for embodied writing that will be "carried by voice, by rhythm" beyond settled significations, beyond the quietude of the written sentence. Not one meaning, but the generation of multiple possibilities—the place where language succeeds because it cannot settle with definition.

Let us reconsider here an often quoted passage from "Laugh of the Medusa": "Text: my body—shot through with streams of song . . . what touches you, the equivoice that affects you, fills your breast with an urge to come to language and launches your force; the rhythm that laughs you; the intimate recipient who makes all metaphors possible and desirable . . ." (252). What Cixous is describing here, and herself enacting through her own language, is a mode of writing, a text, infused with the oral, phonic resonances of language. And her purpose is to open writing to its full metaphoric possibilities; the way one sound suggests another, reminds us of something else, even beyond the intended reference of the word. The ramifications of this phonic, metaphoric process for critical thought are inestimable, for they not only shift theory away from a search for essences, but set loose a dynamic language within the writing of theory that will always keep it moving through and beyond any settled conceptions.

In this sense, the sonorous effects of writing move well beyond what can be *heard* in language and thought. Sound stimulates other sensatory modes of expression and response. Heard messages are tactile, reverberating in ear, mouth, mind. Words become kinetic, moving on and beyond the page. Thought resembles less the stable and staid intellect, more the rhythms of a breathing body. Even perception and vision must accommodate the kinesis of the body. My favorite example of how a moving body can be *seen* as a somatic message comes from an account retold by Walter Ong from a study of Central African oral culture: when a man was asked his assessment of a new village school principal, he replied, "'Let's watch a little how he dances'" (55).[2] Providing a feminist twist to this story, dancer and choreographer Elizabeth Dempster recalls this villager's statement to describe how women's bodies are written and seen in dance: she entitles her essay "Women Writing the Body: Let's Watch a Little How She Dances." To "write the body," as I read Cixous, is to engage in this kind of watching, this keen awareness that movement, sound, sight, touch are all components of language and thought, expression and critical assessment.

We might consider Luce Irigaray's critique of the specularizing disposition of philosophy and theory as a deliberate turn toward sonorous language that ushers us into expansive sensatory modes of theorizing. Rejecting what she calls "the predominance of the visual, and of the discrimination and individualization of form" as "particularly foreign to female eroticism" (*This Sex* 26), she talks about "hearing" and "listening" to writing, as if we were listening "with another ear" or with "ears half-open for what is in such close touch with itself that it confounds your discretion" (29, 118).

Like Cixous, Irigaray has been roundly criticized for making too general claims about women's language and eroticism, but as with my remarks on Cixous, I would call attention here specifically to Irigaray's engagement with sound. When she describes listening to words with "ears half-open," she too—like Trinh, like Griffin—turns away from language that communicates fully, definitively, with ringing clarity. Her theory recalls sounds that work to destabilize thought, not reify the single correct narrative. In this sense, Irigaray's attempts to uncover a "feminine language" actually release its multiple significations even as she would define, and potentially confine, this language as "feminine." And the release comes through sound: "Open your lips; don't open them simply. I don't open them simply. . . . Between our lips, yours and mine, several voices, several ways of speaking resound endlessly, back and forth . . ." (*This Sex* 209). Here theory becomes voices resounding endlessly, much like the voices identified by Pagels in the gnostic gospels, crying out from and within everyone. Theory becomes sound emanating from within language, seeping through its otherwise staid substance and surface. Irigaray says to her intimate respondent: "You are moving. You never stay still. You never stay. . . . What will make that current flow into words? . . . These streams are without fixed banks, this body without fixed boundaries. This unceasing mobility" (214–15).

Bodies, like sound, signal motion in language, and in the process generate mobile significations within writing. This is not a question of "anatomy," Irigaray insists. She chooses instead the notion of "morphology," the different shaping of language from within, from interior contours instead of exterior vision. Her remarks remind me of Walter Ong's description of the "interiority" of oral cultures, their immersion in sound. As he explains, "Sight isolates, sound incorporates. Whereas sight situates the observer outside what he views, at a distance, sound pours into the hearer" (72). Thus in a "sound-dominated verbal economy," he suggests, aggregative and interiorizing tendencies prevail; whereas in visually based communication, analytic and dissecting tendencies emerge: "A typical visual ideal is clarity and distinctness, a

taking apart (Descartes' campaigning for clarity and distinctness regis-
tered an intensification of vision in the human sensorium) . . ." (72–73).
Yet sonorous language can also unfold in a seriotemporal fashion, one
word emerging from the sound of another, syntax itself moving like a
musical score. Thus Irigaray's description of "listening" to language so
that we can *"hear what it says.* That it is continuous, compressible,
dilatable, viscous, conductible, diffusable . . ." (*This Sex* 111).

Given her extensive critiques of specular economies of thought
and language, it is no wonder that Irigaray should turn instead to the
sonorous and kinetic suggestibility of language, particularly the ways
that sound can erupt and disrupt from within. She stays inside language, redeploying its effects, by insistently remaining within the body.
Thus Judith Butler suggests that Irigaray's "textual practice is not
grounded in a rival ontology, but inhabits—indeed penetrates, occupies,
and redeploys—the paternal language itself" (*Bodies* 45). I would only
emphasize that it manages this feat through the disrupting reverberations of sound. As Irigaray herself claims of "woman" and her
language, *"sound* is propagated in her at an astonishing rate. . . . And
meaning would have to be diffused at a speed identical to that of sound
in order for all forms of envelopes . . . to become null and void in the
transmission of 'messages'" (112).

As I read her, Irigaray is acutely attuned to the transmission of
messages, but messages that have not been stripped of their sounding
resonances and intimations, or that have been, as she says, "so clogged
with meaning(s), that they are closed to what does not in some way
echo the already heard" (113). Trinh offers much the same complaint
about the predominance of an instrumental language that works only
"to send out *an unambiguous message,*" language that is prized by the
"voice of literacy": "Clarity is a means of subjugation, a quality both of
official, taught language and of correct writing, two old mates of power:
together they flow, together they flower, vertically, to impose an order.
Let us not forget that writers who advocate the instrumentality of
language are often those who cannot or choose not to see the suchness
of things—a language as language—and therefore, continue to preach
conformity to the norms of well-behaved writing . . ." (*Woman* 16–17).
Elsewhere, she links such language with the "specular structure of
hegemonic discourse and its scopic economy which, according to
Western feminist critiques, circularly bases its in-sights on the sight (a
voyeur's *theoria*) rather than touch" (*Moon* 4).[3]

How might we understand messages that veer away from clarity,
whose meanings are diffused like soundwaves, are "compressible,
dilatable, viscous"? Irigaray ends her essay "The Mechanics of Fluids,"

from which I have just been quoting, with this hint: "And if, by chance, you were to have the impression of not having yet understood everything, then perhaps you would do well to leave your ears half-open for what is in such close touch with itself that it confounds your discretion" (118). Her words prompt me to suggest that much feminist theory invites us to understand its messages with "ears half-open," listening for what is said directly, *and* what remains unsaid, intimated, perhaps purposefully kept secret so that our desire to know is never extinguished by the rush of clogged, clear statements. Such understandings, such sonorous responses to writing, may well confound our discretion, but it is a discretion well worth confounding and complicating, a discretion that always makes space for the flow and kinesis of thought.

A sounding critical language may not constitute the only vehicle for sustaining the necessary multiple and shifting significations required of critical thought. But feminist calls to write the body, I believe, have ushered sounds into critical writing that result in remarkable destabilizations of thinking practices. So much so, that I have come to regard these sounding destabilizations in terms of Julia Kristeva's "semiotic" dispositions in language, the eruption of rhythms and sounds and pulsations that resist the cohesive syntax of a "symbolic order" of language and thought. Kristeva suggests that semiotic dispositions accompany certain crises, specifically "crises within social structures and institutions—the moments of their mutation, evolution, revolution, or disarray" (*Desire* 125). I would suggest that the emergence of oral, phonic, embodied language within feminist theory signals precisely the remarkable disarray within and mutation of contemporary critical thought.

The effects of sound and sonorous language within Kristeva's own theories of language play no small part in this critical destabilization. In her essay "From One Identity to Another," she elaborates some of the forces and effects of semiotic language, in particular the ways in which this language fuels "a *heterogeneousness* to meaning and signification" that can be detected "in the first echolalias of infants as rhythms and intonations anterior to the first phonemes, morphemes, lexemes, and sentences," that can also be "reactivated as rhythms, intonations, glossalalias in psychotic discourse," and that "produces in poetic language 'musical' but also nonsense effects that destroy not only accepted beliefs and significations, but, in radical experiments, syntax itself . . ." (*Desire* 133). The "rhythmic, intonational repetitions" characteristic of semiotic language, Kristeva explains, are always "near the instinctual drives' body; it is a sonorous distinctiveness . . ." (135).

Yet the semiotic does not constitute a separate order of language all its own (except perhaps in extreme psychotic discourse). Instead, Kristeva regards semiotic and symbolic dispositions as part of a "bipolar economy" that can combine "in different ways to constitute *types of discourse*, types of signifying practices" (134). Scientific discourse, for example, would tend "to reduce as much as possible the semiotic component," while poetic language would engage and often exploit the semiotic disposition. While Kristeva sees the semiotic and symbolic functions of language continually interacting within prevailing signifying practices, she suggests some historical demarcations between these two modes of language when she describes how the semiotic reenacts for the "modern community" the "practice that the materialists of antiquity unsuccessfully championed against the ascendance of theoretical reason" (*Desire* 147).

Kristeva's ideas recall for me Eric Havelock's similar arguments about the different dispositions of oral and written language that he identifies when discussing the transition from orality to literacy in early Greek culture. As he explains, the oral world of early Greeks was infused with sonorous pulsations and body rhythms through which thought emerged. They formed the very medium of poetry, the most valued and sacred language, and necessarily connected to the "motor responses of the human body" (72). But with the advent of writing, the rhythms and sounds of poetic language—as a vehicle of thought—gave way to the staid essences of philosophy. Exit Homer. Enter Plato. And with this change, we have the movement away from sound and toward sight, away from body and toward mind, away from a concrete, dynamic language—the "overlapping meanings" in early Greek drama—to writing filled with abstraction and fact—the "language of theoretic analysis" (15). Havelock's story of the birth of western philosophy may seem familiar to many feminists who have also described the deprecation of the body in western systems of thought. But his account of how this deprecation of the body is directly connected to the repression of sound in language bears an eerie resemblance to contemporary feminist calls about writing the body into theory.

Andrea Nye, though writing in different contexts, describes how Plato's ideal language seeks "the bare bones of truth" and turns away from "the fleshy fat of ordinary language" (33). Her bodily metaphors suggest the connection between truth and bare bones that has subsequently come to inform theoretical traditions. Philosophy works to strip language of its potentially multiple meanings, exposing the bone; while the ambiguous messages of Greek drama, by contrast, were fueled by what Havelock called the "overlapping meanings which verged on contradiction, a manner which could be said to reflect the ad hoc empiricism of orality as opposed to the consistent clarity of literate conceptualism" (15).

What did this rhythmic, bodily language sound like? Curiously, the examples Havelock chooses are those passages—committed to writing during the time when oral narrative was being set to the page— that describe women in motion. The first is from a Homeric hymn to Aphrodite, in which we can still hear the dynamic language of life and process and motion: "'whither the humid force of blowing zephyr carried her over the wave of the foam-roaring sea within mollient foam. And her the seasons received welcoming and put ambrosial garments around her and on her immortal head they set a well-fashioned crown [both] beautiful [and] golden . . .'" (107). As Havelock points out, there is little stasis here. Instead of essential forms, we have a language infused with verbs, action, movement, becoming. This same dynamism marks his second example, where Callimachus celebrates Zeus by reciting his birth: "'In Parrhasia it was Rhea bare you, where was a hill sheltered with thickest brush. . . . There your mother had laid you down from her mighty lap, straightway she sought a stream of water, wherewith she might purge her of the soilure of birth and wash your body therein'" (108). Language here, even though forms of "being" are finding their way into expression, is propelled by movement, dynamic flow, concrete action and experience. But such vitality will soon be replaced by a language of permanent entities, ideal states, and static being, one in which the verb "to be" assumes dominance.

Thus Plato: "A poet, whether he is writing epic, lyric, or drama, surely ought always to represent the divine nature as it really is. And the truth is that that nature is good and must be described as such" (46). Or, "Is it not true, then, that things in the most perfect condition are the least affected by changes from the outside? . . . So this immunity to change from outside is characteristic of anything which, thanks to art or nature or both, is in a satisfactory state" (47). I take these citations from Plato's *Republic*, where he criticizes poets for what he perceives as their excessive imagination and expression. About the language of poets, Plato has this to say: "We must also get rid of all that terrifying language, the very sound of which is enough to make one shiver: 'loathsome Styx,' 'the River of Wailing,' 'infernal spirits,' 'anatomies,' and so on. . . . So we will have none of it; and we shall encourage writing in the opposite strain" (50). With this writing "in the other strain," we have not only the birth of essential truth and good, of facts and theories, but of the discourses that grew from the status and stasis of writing: philosophy, history, science. No wonder Havelock surmises: "When [Plato] turns against poetry it is precisely its dynamism, its fluidity, its concreteness, its particularity, that he deplores. He could not have reached the point of deploring it if he had not become literate himself" (96).

If with Plato we encounter a shift away from a dynamic poetic language, "that terrifying language, the very sound of which is enough to make one shiver," then I suggest that feminist calls to write the body signal a reiteration of that very language into theory. I say this not to endorse some revisionist historical narrative about the development of western philosophy (though I personally find Havelock's account as fascinating as Pagels and her accounts of the gnostic gospels), but to call attention to the crucial effects of sound in the shaping and reshaping of theory. We cannot understand the dynamics of body writing without appreciating how the body serves as a conduit of sound, the very sounds that Plato found so frightening, sounds that threatened to destabilize the philosophical essences which he sought to define.

But why should a sounding language become so threatening? And why is it that theory, in particular, came to rely on clear vision as a model of thought rather than the resonances of sound? In tracing his historical scenario, Havelock describes how Aristotle believed philosophy had its beginnings in visual response to thought. Thus the words Aristotle used to describe the intellectual enterprise of his Lyceum were "*theoria* and its verb *theorein*, both referring to the act of looking at something." Havelock surmises, "Why choose vision as the metaphor for an intellectual operation, unless guided by the subconscious recognition that the operation had arisen out of viewing the written word rather than just hearing it spoken?" (111).

Writing here and now, in the contexts of feminist theory rather than Greek philosophy, I'm tempted to alter the terms of Havelock's statement. I would ask, when noting the remarkable emphasis on sound in the theory of Cixous, Irigaray, and Kristeva: why choose sound as a metaphor for an intellectual operation, unless guided by the recognition that the operation had arisen out of hearing the written word rather than just seeing it on the page? Indeed Kristeva describes the semiotic disposition of language "according to the Greek *sémeion* . . . a *distinctiveness* admitting of an uncertain and indeterminate articulation" because it does not refer "to a signified object for a thetic consciousness. . . ." She goes on to relate how Plato's *Timeus* speaks of a "*chora*" or "receptacle" that remained "unnameable, improbable, hybrid, anterior to naming, to the One, to the father, and consequently, maternally connoted to such an extent that its merits not even the rank of syllable'" (*Desire* 133).

If such semiotic disruptions are continually at work within prevailing signifying practices, then I believe we should specifically inquire into their effects in the recent disarray and mutations occurring within critical theory. Let me return briefly to Irigaray, not for an example of semiotic language that runs away entirely from the "thetic consciousness" and regulated symbolic meanings described by Kristeva, but one that engages that kind of "uncertain and inde-terminate articulation" *within* the parameters of critical thought. I turn to Irigaray's specific critical and amorous response to the work of a major male philosopher. In her book *Marine Lover of Friedrich Nietzsche,* she speaks directly to Nietzsche, her voice the vehicle of her writing. But Irigaray's voice here does not simply represent a highly vocalized, aural mode of writing. Rather, she claims her voice as the very substance, the very bodily matter, which through its repression made Nietzsche's own writing possible: "But, had I never held back, never would you have remembered that something exists which has a language other than your own. That, from her prison, someone was calling out to return to the air. That your words reasoned all the better because within them a voice was captive. Amplifying your speech with an endless resonance" (3).

Here is a voice writing from within thetic consciousness, within theoretical traditions, and setting loose its very speech "with an endless resonance." Contrasted with the more conventional critical prose that Irigaray adopted in her *Speculum of the Other Woman,* a work that also set out to respond to male philosophical traditions, Irigaray's writing in *Marine Lover* is lyrical, amorous, fused with the poetic sounds. It unsettles not through opposition, but love; it does not overthrow, but mutates. Something is cracking open. But the resulting articulation is tenuous, not clear and pronounced. She is too intimate with Nietzsche to have it otherwise. And articulations are carried, continually, through sound and hearing:

> Yes, yes, yes . . . I hear you. And I do not hear you. I am your hearing. Between you and yourself, I ensure the vocal medium. A perpetual relay between your mouth and your ear. Go on, I am singing your memory so that you do not fall into some abyss of forgetfulness. (3)

Irigaray adopts a special positioning for her writing—in language, and in Nietzsche's philosophy. For as a woman, she has already been inscribed there; and now, as a critic, she writes from that place of inscription, as the very body and sounds that he held captive. But she knows full well that she has also been the object of his love and longing, the captive to which he might return. She releases the sonorous language which makes this return possible. In a section entitled "The Song of the Cicada," this return is described as a descent into woman's silence, a silence that resounds with something he wants: "And might it not be she whom you come back to seek at night? The persistence of a silence that would not be obedience" (39). I take this silence to be a massive source of vocal instigation, something large and vacuous like the "O," Broumas's "cave of sound," to which the male philosopher returns for sustenance, a linguistic and sexual fix, or as Irigaray says, "the nostalgia for woman that you preach and that haunts you beyond your resolves."

But Irigaray herself is turning this nostalgia into a different song, not the pure semiotic disruption that he seeks like the sirens' wailings from the ocean, not the sounds produced when "she sings endlessly, filling the air with plenteous profusion, without ever speaking or breaking" (39), but a critical articulation made up of this very sonorous substance. Words usher from body, resonating from mouth to ear. Theory articulates itself from the very body and sounds that fueled Nietzsche's wild proclamations.

Because, strangely enough, the modalities of Irigaray's writing are not far from Nietzsche's, though tapped and used for such disparate purposes. One might well argue that Nietzsche's writing is filled with maddening sounds and voices. Irigaray's, by contrast, is a quiet love letter, seeping into and through his loud utterances. I am hardly one who will claim that only women can write the body, or that the written body is always female, or that oral evocation of bodily language can be simplistically sexed. Nonetheless, the peculiar sounds of language carried through mouth and ear, sounds that Irigaray sets loose *within her own thetic consciousness*, and in direct response to a powerful philosopher, do indeed signal, I believe, a mutation of theory facilitated through feminist critique.

Such semiotic dispositions and disruptions within theoretical writing need not necessarily be purely amorous or infused with lush, lyrical prose. Let us take Kristeva herself as an example of something different, yet similarly disruptive. In her essay "Stabat Mater," she divides her page in half, using one column for her analytic reflections and writings about the cultural consignment of the Virgin Mary, and the other to explore her own poetic inscriptions of giving birth to her son. Both discourses provide critical commentary on language, among other matters. Yet one voice maintains literate decorum, theoretical precision, while the other lets go, resonates: In both discourses, we encounter the female body, but only the second gives us body writing: "Words that are always too distant, too abstract for this underground swarming of seconds, folding in unimaginable spaces. . . . Laugh. Impossible. Flash on the unnameable, weavings of abstractions to be torn. Let a body venture at last out of its shelter, take a chance with meaning under a veil of words. WORD FLESH" (*Reader* 162).

At this site, and *within* her theoretical writing, Kristeva seizes the sensations of sonorous language, all the instinctive bodily energies of semiotic disruptions: "Taut eardrum, tearing sound out of muted silence. Wind among grasses, a seagull's faraway call, echoes of waves, auto horns, voices, or nothing? Or his own tears, my newborn, spasm of syncopated void. I no longer hear anything, but the eardrum keeps transmitting this resonant vertigo to my skull, the hair" (166–67).

I am of course very interested in these effects of language resonating between eardrum and skull and hair, all the more because they differ in tone and context from Irigaray's otherwise similar language resonating between mouth and ear. Is Kristeva's engagement in body writing peculiar to a woman giving birth, to the pre-oedipal sonorous connection between mother and child? Earlier I cited Kristeva's association of the semiotic with the Greek *sémeion*, with that which remains "unnameable, improbable, hybrid, anterior to naming, to the One, to the father, and consequently, maternally connoted. . . ." I bring up this question of maternal connotations because Kristeva has been criticized for her ideas about pre-oedipal language and maternal inscriptions.[4] And my own ideas about the semiotic disposition of feminist calls to write the body can hardly escape related suspicions that they potentially play into an uncritical embrace of the maternal body.

Indeed the whole topic of "Writing and Motherhood," to use Susan Suleiman's term, has generated both compelling and contentious theories about the possibility of inscribing maternity into the order of culture and language. Suleiman's essay is one of several in the collection *The (M)other Tongue* that calls attention to feminist psycho-analytic theories about language, especially the possible articulations of sonorous pre-oedipal language—those rhythms and pulsations of the very earliest communication between mother and child—and the surfacings of this language in various forms of art and writing (352–77). At their most promising, I believe, and as Kristeva's own literary and art criticism demonstrate, these surfacings can help us come to terms with what Carolyn Burke calls "the question of the maternal at the level of language," (113) perhaps as part of, or configured with, the emergence of the semiotic, poetic, and oral at the level of writing.[5]

But retrievals of maternal language bring back all the ghosts of repression and their feminine associations, not to mention a series of other questions that haunt the inquiry. Does sonorous language necessarily derive from maternal forces, or constitute an expression of maternal desire? Is recourse to pre-oedipal language the exclusive domain of feminist writers, or women writers (something Kristeva would emphatically deny)? Do turns to maternal language only betray a desperate attempt to seek refuge in the soothing embrace of the mother within the ravages of patriarchy? These kinds of questions, and more, have troubled inquiries into the maternal dimensions of language, and must necessarily effect my reading of Kristeva's own heavily weighted maternal connotation in her theories of language.

And yet, I believe, there are ways to proceed with such an inquiry without invoking maternal language as some salvation from patriarchal discourse. Recognizing that the mother tongue has become a powerful and problematic metaphor for feminists does not necessarily entail that we shun it altogether. It comes as no surprise to me that many feminist critics have turned to the figures of mother and mother tongues to elaborate a different kind and quality of writing. Nor is it surprising that feminist discourse itself has relied on the grand metaphors of father and mother to articulate the workings of systems of oppression. The striving for a different language, for alternative modes of writing, may work through the maternal metaphor because this striving is for a more fully embodied language, and the mother's body provides rich resources for such an undertaking. Bodies, after all, can be more than simplistic womblike encampments of comfort and desire. They can also become resources for the reworking of words, sounds, meanings.

Consider, for example, Trinh's reflections on "certain women's womb writing, which neither separates the body from the mind nor sets the latter against the heart (an attitude that would lead us back to the writing-as-birth-delivering-labor concept and to the biologico-metaphorization of women's bodies previously discussed) but allows each part of the body to become infused with consciousness" (40). Or consider how Cixous draws on a similar configuration when she describes the peculiar phonic qualities of women's writing, and claims that "a woman is never far from 'mother,' . . . I don't mean the overbearing, clutchy 'mother' but, rather, what touches you, the equivoice that affects you, fills your breast with an urge to come to language and launches your force; the rhythm that laughs you; the intimate recipient who makes all metaphors possible and desirable; body (body? bodies?) . . ." ("Laugh" 252).

In her "Cyborg Manifesto," Donna Haraway, often critical of invocations of the mother in feminist criticism, chooses metaphors of regeneration rather than birth, and leaves us with the image of the salamander. She explains that for salamanders "regeneration after injury" involves regrowth of the injured body part, accompanied by the possibility of other twining growths and productions at the site of the wound. Calling for a ceaselessly inventive politics of regeneration, Haraway writes: "We have all been injured, profoundly. We require regeneration, not rebirth . . ." (*Simians* 181).

When maternal reproduction threatens to become excessive, transgressive, out of control, it is often figured as monstrous, a favorite metaphor of Haraway's that she uses to describe potential transformations. I would link the semiotic dispositions in language and all their sounding, pulsating rhythms with this maternal-turned-monstrous potential of writing—the ability to generate, from *within* the injured body of language, new productions that reshape the very body of critical thought. After all, invocations of maternal language in feminist theory are often more provoking than comforting, more about taking risks with language than finding comfort in some womblike world of symbiosis. "I don't mean the overbearing, clutchy 'mother,'" Cixous reminds us, "but, rather, what touches you, fills your breast with an urge to come to language. . . ."

And so we must ask: What happens when such launching, rhythmic language infuses various modes of "thetic" writing—as Cixous insists it must, and as Trinh insists when she engages body writing as "that abstract-concrete, personal-political realm of excess not fully contained by writing's unifying structural forces," where its "physicality (vocality, tactility, touch, resonance), or edging and margin, exceeds the rationalized 'clarity' of communicative structures and cannot be fully explained by any analysis" (*Woman* 44). What happens when the bodily energies of the semiotic, of the oral and phonic, infuse the discourse of theory?

Here is where I come back to Kristeva's ideas about the emergence of semiotic dispositions at times of "crisis within social structures and institutions—the moments of their mutation, evolution, revolution, or disarray." It seems to me that the emergence of embodied, sonorous, disruptive, and potentially regenerative language within theoretical writing marks a distinctive feminist mutation. Kristeva suggests that it is "probably necessary to be a woman . . . not to renounce theoretical reason but to compel it to increase its power by giving it an object beyond its limits." She goes on to explain how such a position "provides a possible basis for a theory of signification, which, confronted with poetic language, could not in any way account for it, but would rather use it as an indication of what is heterogeneous to meaning . . ." (*Desire* 146).

I want to suggest that this is exactly how feminist critics who bring body and sound to writing "use" language: as an indication of what is heterogeneous to meaning, an indication of how words suggest more than they say, how a sounding language seeps through and beyond the ostensibly sealed surface of signification, intimates another, and another, idea. And I suggest that feminists do this "not to renounce theoretical reason but to compel it to increase its power. . . ."

As a conduit of sound, the body in language unsettles meaning, to the point of crisis. The vocal instigations stirring up this crisis resonate throughout feminist theory, its keen ear and taut eardrum, its intellectual commitment to unruly sounds.

Coda

When I first began to ponder connections between sonorous language and feminist critical thought, the body emerged as a kind of linchpin, linking the two discourses through their mutual reliance on somatic articulation. At that time, some years ago, feminist critics tended to agree on what constituted the female body.

How things have changed.

In her essay on a "Politics of Location," Adrienne Rich called for a "moratorium on saying 'the body,'" and urged instead an attention to particular bodies and lived experience (215). But were even these particular bodies firm, unchangeable substances? Elizabeth Grosz shifts the inquiry further by questioning the generalized association of women and body, arguing that specific bodies are "volatile" and continually inscribed, constituted, produced: bodies are the material of the "mobile and changing terms of cultural production" (*Volatile Bodies* x–xi). In the work of Judith Butler, bodies continue to become destabilized. Butler shows that such bodies "matter" all the more because of the subjective determinations and "regulatory norms" that are always shaping them (*Bodies* 22). Neither women's nor lesbians' bodies are fixed entities. Queer bodies evidence the volatility, dangers, and possibilities of ongoing bodily constructions.

When one writes the body, then, exactly which body is being written? Whose sounding language is invoked? In the chapters that follow, I listen for critical sounds connected to very specific bodies that have emerged, changed, and themselves mutated within feminist theory. Dealing with volatile bodies should by no means obscure the precise and precarious conjunction of word and ear, thought and tongue. To the contrary, such changeability shows that what Butler calls "enabling disruptions" (23) can occur at a variety of shifting sites—in bodies, in language, in the social fabric. The very recognition of the body's volatility may well have derived from the engagement with body writing and its release of an unsettling somatic language. If so, then feminist efforts to write the body have loosened the ground, as it were, thus facilitating many of the productive destabilizations and disruptions of normative thought that have shaken intellectual traditions in recent years.

And so I turn now to the specific and changing bodies that have come to proliferate within feminist theory. These "tongue-like forms" and "big red mouths" move language, with bodies, through the vital process of critical mutation. In the present chapter, I describe the crisis that signals this movement. In what follows, I listen for the resulting articulations.

4

Queer Curves

There is more to the story of bodies and sound. If, in tracing the sounds of critical language, we begin with O, then we must now follow the sensuous paths that Olga Broumas describes when she invites us to let the mind move "along / the slopes / of the faithful body," as she defines her own task in this movement of language:

> I work
> in silver the tongue-like forms
> that curve round a throat
>
> an arm-pit, the upper
> thigh, whose significance stirs in me
> like a curviform alphabet. . . . (23)

What can it mean to write such "tongue-like forms," to bring into critique the erotic dimensions of language as it curves with the body? Beginning her essay on the possibilities of "Refiguring Lesbian Desire," Elizabeth Grosz takes notice of the "exceptionally powerful and worthwhile" mass of criticism recently emerging in the field of lesbian and gay studies. Yet in this particular essay, she wants to write something different, something "wildly speculative" and "openly experimental" that might "welcome unknown readings, new claims, provocative analyses" and the language it thrives on—critical, desirous, intensely embodied. Explaining how sexuality and desire might help us seize possibilities for relation, movement, connection, she writes:

> The sites most intensely invested always occur at a conjunction . . .
> they are always surface effects between one thing and another—
> between a hand and a breast, a tongue and a cunt, a mouth and
> food, a nose and a rose. (78)

Pondering these bodily "transmutations," Grosz poses these questions: "What is it that together, in parts and bits and interconnections, we can make that is new, that is exploratory, that opens up further spaces, induces further intensities, speeds up, enervates, and proliferates production (production of the body, production of the world)?" (80–81).

And, I would add, production of the word. In this chapter I want to pose exactly these kinds of questions about the transmutation of lesbian and queer bodies within feminist theory. What peculiar nexus of body and thought emerges, and proliferates, here? If, as I elaborated in the previous chapter, bodies serve as a conduit for sound within the written word, then now I want to trace how that written word utters itself on the page, how it moves as voice and tongue, as Broumas would say, "round a throat / an arm-pit, the upper / thigh. . . ." How is it that these bodies materialize in language—as metaphors, as subjects of intense theoretical discussion, as conduits of vocal expression and thought? And what are the physical, tactile, critical messages carried through this precise movement of words?

In approaching these questions, I find myself turning to those "surface effects between one thing and another" described by Grosz, specifically what I take to be that crucial intersection between bodies and texts—what Judith Butler describes as the continual interchange between "language and materiality" (*Bodies* 68). Within feminist criticism, the writings of lesbian feminists and, more recently, queer theorists have invoked very distinctive bodily desires, tactile sensations and speculations, in critical thought.

Elspeth Probyn might describe this process as an ontological and epistemological move, the way in which "the experiential may enable an enunciative position" that at once reflects a specific sexual identity and moves beyond fixed notions of identity (29). The ontological sense of *being* a lesbian, for instance, might enable a unique mode of enunciation. Yet this enunciation partakes in the shifting, dynamic movement of language and epistemology, moves beyond *being*, and into the moving realm of *becoming*. Both language and bodies proliferate, curve around to something else, somewhere else. Sound emerges not so much as a dominant sensation, but as a catalyst for stirring up "enunciations," for instigating the material, tactile, and kinetic energies of language and thought.

In this curving movement, the way language keeps producing more and more of its surface, skinlike effects, I listen for the sounds of the O in lesbian and queer critical writing. Yet I do not want to obscure the different investments each discourse makes in the body—lesbian feminists tending to embrace a lesbian body as sexually specific and fairly stable; queer theorists paying attention to the constructed nature of such identities and their potential to destabilize the tight hold of heterosexuality. In my own venture to hear the distinctive sounds of language in these and other critical expressions, I find myself impressed with the moving, curving articulations of each—as if words are always rushing beyond their significations, as if language and bodies are always exceeding prescribed limits of both syntax and social norm. In a sense, both discourses bring feminist theory to its discursive limits—to that curve along the skin, the place where thought must bend to accommodate body movement and all its messages.

Consider Elizabeth Meese's self-conscious writing as a lesbian critic, her dexterous enfolding of subject and text, lesbian body and language. In her book *(Sem)Erotics: Theorizing Lesbian : Writing*, she merges the linguistic activity of semiotics with amorous, bodily animation. Distinguishing "between 'writing about' and 'writing with (or as)' one's subject," Meese invites us to become aware of "how one takes one's 'place' in language." She assumes her own place as a lesbian critic so that she can explore the very expansive dimensions of this place. As Meese explains, "I am interested in exploring textual erotics beyond content, acknowledging the blurred boundaries between the personal and the critical, the particular, concrete intimacy of sexual expression, and the (for some) abstract aridity of high theory" (xviii). Just as she "writes about" this language, so she actually engages it as a critic, "searching for the words, syntax and grammar that can articulate the body, my body, and perhaps yours." Her criticism becomes intimate exchange, a kind of "love letter" that loses none of its intellectual vigor yet openly indulges its physical powers of connection: "When I write my love letter to you, I want to bring myself to you, hand myself over. When I write about lesbian : writing, I take my life in my hands, as my text." Her writing moves, "when my tongue slides over the osmotic, lively breathing surfaces of your skin like words," or "as the pen makes its tracks across the body of the page, its friction and its struggle to mark the course faithfully, our passions inscribed energetically in the body of language in the mind: a love letter" (3).

We are not simply talking about bodies here, but very specific bodies that evoke specific rhythms and gestures and tactile sensations in writing, and that bring these sensations to the literate production of knowledge. In my last chapter, I tried to link feminist theories of body writing with the distinctive somatic component of sounding language, and traced the echoes of these sounds in producing a crisis within theory. In Meese's theory, this crisis unfolds at the convergence of hands and text, tongue and page, skin and words—and moves on from there. Voice merges with text, becomes a material component of written language. Literary criticism engages the analyzed text in erotic and tactile ways.

Listen, for instance, to the way Meese ends, or tries to end, her chapter on Virginia Woolf and Vita Sackville-West, addressing letters to both of them:

> Dear Vita and Virginia,
>   How can I read your letters without, above all, wanting to write? Years of correspondence, circulating affection and longing make me desire more letters. I don't want them to end or to stop, so I continue (y)our correspondence.
>   Dear V, Your sheepdog puts her muzzle on her paws and waits at the door. Will you pet her when you arrive? Will you remember the feel of her fur and discover new ways to startle her? Love, V.
>   Dear V and V, I feel empty when I write one without the other. . . . (41)

Reading and criticism have now curved into longing, a desire for more letters, a desire to write *to* these authors as much as *about* them—as if physically connected, though only through words. Yet such physicality does not obscure critical abstraction and analysis. Meese carefully reviews and incorporates into her writing quotations and perspectives of other critics. She is thoroughly academic, thoroughly erotic, thoroughly critical. In fact, critical and erotic connections become absolutely necessary, as they do when Meese begins her chapter "Gertrude Stein and Me": "Yes, I know Gertrude Stein too. I have known her since the day I knew I was a lesbian. I knew both at once, something about the one connecting the other. That is worth understanding in some detail—a lesbian convergence, and here for the first time I bring them together, literally, in the letter" (63).

Yet is this lesbian writing? Is this bodily and tactile investment in literary criticism a peculiarly lesbian undertaking? Meese herself is reluctant to define and thereby essentialize a lesbian writer, and prefers instead to regard lesbian writing not so much as a subject but as an action, as performance and engagement, a vibrant linguistic activity instigated by certain subjects who are continually articulating and inventing themselves in language. Here again I locate the curving of the O. Ontology gives way to epistemological verve; language and bodies and critical thought move. As Meese explains, "The lesbian writer seeks to intervene in language, reinvent, or better, re-work its texture, to produce an exploratory language through which we can find ourselves as subject and (of) desire." Or later, sliding down that same page: "And that word, 'lesbian.' Can you tell me whose word it is? . . . 'Lesbian' is applied to me in a system I do not control, that cannot control itself. Yet it is a word I want to embrace, re-write and re-claim, not to install it but to explode its meaning . . ." (14).

The writing of letters, the continual exchange of words, seems the perfect way to ensure that critical meaning never will be effectively "installed" but always will be unfolding, reverberating. Meese sustains this critical dialogic exchange through letter writing that extends even beyond the boundaries of her book. Her last chapter, entitled "Body Talk," features all the "'extra' letters" that have somehow not found their way into the previous chapters. They rebound, here, at the end, and take us beyond the ending. "Dear L," Meese writes (as she continually addresses her interlocutor throughout the book) in one particular letter, "Through writing I call out the lesbian in me, and in you as you read my letters. Space is opened, between me and the 'I' (of) writing, the discursive subject, between the 'I' on the page and the reader's 'I,' or how/who I imagine her to be. Of course you can decide to read or to put the book down. You agree or disagree, defining a lesbian reader as you go. Together, we create templates, texts, for lesbian : love" (137). Writing, like spoken language, does not stop to rest, does not stop for more than momentary confirmation, before rushing on to another thought, a response, and then another response. Meese ends her book by refusing a strict ending, by inviting letters: "If enough people send me letters, perhaps I can collect them. Writing produces more writing. This story of lesbian : love starts and starts again. . . . Why don't you write me when you get a chance. Then you'll understand what a 'lesbian' is, the secret involved in writing : lesbian—'(. . . . . .)'. I'm hoping for a reply. (A loveletter would be nice.) Yours, L" (138).

This very multiplication of letters and resulting generation of messages unfold like soundwaves, and need to be read for all their mobile meanings. Meese shows us, through her own sonorous and sensual language, how placing oneself as a lesbian in writing hardly means ascribing to some fixed message or even to a defined sexuality. Far from that, identity becomes process, a shift described by Shane Phelan as a movement from *being* to *becoming*. Phelan asks: "What relations of power are called into play when we assume a 'lesbian' subject position? Which of those relations require change, and which might be drawn upon to effect that change?" (55). In Meese's criticism, these assumptions and relations and effects materialize in writing. They call into play questions about how we read, how texts present themselves to us and we to them, how literary meanings can and do shift through the convergence of bodies in critical writing.

ⓖ

"So the poem became your language?"

"Yes. . . . Everything was like a poem, with different curves, different levels. . . . I had an image of trying to reach something around a corner. . . ."

—"An Interview: Audre Lorde and Adrienne Rich" (82–84)

We might inquire, then, into the larger dimensions of this convergence, and ask how lesbian critics have made language into a somatic, even poetic, vehicle of critical reassessment and change. I would turn first to Monique Wittig, whose critique of fixed categories of sexuality and gender make it possible for her to claim the word "lesbian" as curving beyond the "straight mind." For in this straight epistemology, as she explains, the very "categories of language" force us "to speak of ourselves and to conceive of ourselves as women and as men," and in so doing make us "instrumental in maintaining heterosexuality" (*Straight Mind* 30). What's worse is that these categories continually inscribe themselves in discourses, so that the very language we speak and write continually reflects the unquestioned assumption "that what founds society, any society, is heterosexuality."

Wittig's own writing, both as novelist and critic, works to construct lesbian bodies even as it dismantles the very categories that have nominally inscribed their existence. And she does this through a sounding, curving language, one which dismantles what Jeffner Allen calls the "wedge" that has separated poetry and philosophy, and destabilizes the "laws of gender-marked syntax and semantics" ("Poetic Politics" 314). As Allen explains, this destabilization derives from the release of sounding poetic rhythms which, in Wittig's language, urge on "female syntax and semantics to write that which has been without words" (313).

We can hear these sounds unleashed in the beginning of *The Lesbian Body* as Wittig bids farewell to the old order of inscribed, categorical bodies: "In this dark adored adorned gehenna say your farewells m/y very beautiful one m/y very strong one m/y very indomitable one m/y very learned one m/y very ferocious one m/y very gentle one m/y best beloved to what they, the women, call affection tenderness or gracious abandon. . . . Not one will be able to bear seeing you with eyes turned up lids cut off your yellow smoking intestines spread in the hollow of your hands your tongue spat from your mouth long green strings of bile flowing over your breast, not one will be able to bear your low frenetic insistent laughter" (15).

Here body writing emerges with a vengeance—at once turning on language, and turning and twisting within it to produce something different. Elaine Marks describes Wittig's writing as a version of "lesbian intertextuality": "The female body, whose every part is enumerated, destroyed, and reassembled is the alpha and omega of Wittig's fiction" (289). But this intertextuality, I want to insist, is also the alpha and omega of Wittig's criticism and theory. Consider Wittig's essays in *The Straight Mind*, where her own language is admittedly more tame, but where the dynamic energies and excessive meanings of language become her volatile critical subject. Honing in on the concrete, material quality of language, she describes its continual movement in and beyond meaning, ultimately producing not "one meaning," but "polysemy" (67). Wittig's complaint is that women are written into language, already inscribed "into language through gender" (81). Her answer: "Gender must be destroyed. The possibility of its destruction is given through the very exercise of language. . . . To destroy the categories of sex in politics and in philosophy, to destroy gender in language . . . is therefore part of my work in writing, as a writer" (80).

Posed as a critic, Wittig describes this process at work in her novel: "The bar in the *j/e* of *The Lesbian Body* is a sign of excess. A sign that helps to imagine an excess of 'I,' and 'I' exalted. 'I' has become so powerful in *The Lesbian Body* that it can attack the order of heterosexuality in texts and assault the so-called love, the heroes of love, and lesbianize them, lesbianize the symbols, lesbianize the gods and the goddesses, lesbianize the men and the women. This 'I' can be destroyed in the attempt and resuscitated. Nothing resists this 'I' (or this *tu*, which is its same, its love), which spreads itself in the whole world of the book, like a lava flow that nothing can stop" (*Straight Mind* 87). Almost paradoxically, the image of the fractured "I" must be seen, on the page, even as its effect is to "spread itself in the whole world of the book." But this is an image that forces a conjunction of vision and kinesis, stirred up by the excessive rhythms and reverberations of somatic language. The splitting of *j/e* unleashes within language the very sonorous forces that transmogrify writing. Instead of establishing categories and fixing meaning, this writing works to unhinge just those structures, such as gender and heterosexuality, into which we have been inscribed. Lesbian is no longer a category, but a process, to lesbianize, to release from categorical inscription.

Wittig strikes me as being fascinated by those energies in language that keep it on the move, that follow its curves along sounds and bodies. Perhaps this is why she is drawn to Nathalie Sarraute's writing

and its preoccupation with "'l'usage de la parole' [the use of speech]"
(*Straight Mind* 91). Sarraute's works are filled, as Wittig explains, with
"interlocutors," with all their "interventions," "changes of meaning,"
and "variations" that prevent any single interpretation. In this way they
function "contrary to Plato's Socrates" for whom dialogue was really
only monologue. With Sarraute, the pace is too fast, the exchange too
incessant, to settle on one meaning. Wittig herself seizes this pace in her
own critical language: "I would delight in speaking of the very
substance of the text itself, of the rhythm, the sequences, and their mode
of development, of the use of words dispersing between interlocutors,
of the spectacular oscillations of the text at moments when shifts in
point of view take place, of the interlocutory sequences, of the clichés
that are orchestrated around a word, as though by baton, of the birth
and deployment in counterpoint of a text" (92). Not surprisingly, she
describes these dynamics as resembling a "kind of Greek choir," the
place where the rhythms of oral language can enjoy their most frenzied
expression. Of course there is also "locution," the statement of the single
"I" as she stakes out a claim to definition and meaning. Yet Wittig
always seems drawn to the other force in language, or to what she calls
in Sarraute's novels the "double movement" of the two modes. Here the
ceaseless exchange of speech, reverberating in writing, would, as Wittig
explains, continually prevent "organization into a system of compulsory meaning" (100). Or, we might say, they continually interrupt
straightness in language, which continually curves, twists, crosses over
into and through itself, turns into something else.

©

> The word 'queer' itself means *across*—it comes from the Indo-European
> root -*twerkw*, which also yields the German *quer* (transverse), Latin
> *torquere* (to twist), English *athwart*.
>
> —Eve Sedgwick, *Tendencies* (xii)

     How is feminist theory invested in the curves and crossings of
bodies, sound, and language? For certain theorists, this investment has
been substantial, and has helped shape a field of theory consumed with
bodies that portend changes across language and sexualities. Their
criticism occupies a distinctive place in the terrain of the queer. In the
particular examples of feminist lesbian and queer theory that I explore
here, I want to listen for the destabilizing sounds that transform bodies
through a lively critical language that at once pays precise attention to
and runs away from categorical inscriptions of sex. The lesbian body

becomes a subject of analysis even as it becomes a body that changes analysis. Thus Jacques Lacan's "Signification of the Phallus" becomes Judith Butler's "The Lesbian Phallus," even as such critical essays and subjects can move in different directions, along the curves of different bodies, historical and imagined.

Language plays no small part in this inquiry into bodies and their potential crossings and transformations. As Butler explains, the continual bearing of matter and language on each other forms the catalyst for what might function as a crucial "enabling disruption" and "resignification" within the norms of heterosexuality (*Bodies* 23, 240). Such resignifications would not overthrow the heterosexual order and all of its supporting discourses (and thereby run the risk of instituting yet another exclusive system of sexuality and discourses), but rather cross and disrupt it from within.

I want to suggest that within the terrain of queer theory, lesbian critics and a variety of queer feminists are prompting exactly these kinds of disruptions and resignifications within critical theory. My point is simply that if bodies do matter in the ongoing symbolic production of sexualities and in the shaping of culture, then they obviously also matter in the production and reshaping of theory. Consider Butler's own expressed reservations about her engagement with theory in a traditional sense: "And what's worse, I do not understand the notion of 'theory,' and am hardly interested in being cast as its defender, much less in being signified as part of an elite gay/lesbian theory crowd that seeks to establish the legitimacy of gay/lesbian studies within the academy. Is there a pregiven distinction between theory, politics, culture, media? How do those divisions operate to quell a certain intertextual writing that might well generate wholly different epistemic maps?" (14).

Her concept and practice of "a certain intertextual writing" signals the breakdown of those very structures that demarcate not only such discourses as theory, politics, and poetry, but the numerous kinds of identity categories that establish what is in and out, male and female, heterosexual and homosexual. As Diana Fuss explains in her introductory essay to *Inside/Out*, "The fear of the homo, which continually *rubs up against* the hetero (tribadic-style), concentrates and codifies the very real possibility and ever-present threat of a collapse of boundaries, an effacing of limits, and a radical confusion of identities" (6). Theory here exists at the very crossroads of its own demarcations. Butler continues her thoughts on this subject: "If the political task is to show that theory is never merely *theoria*, in the sense of disengaged contemplation, and to insist that it is fully political (*phronesis* or even *praxis*), than why not simply call this operation *politics*, or some necessary permutation of it?" (14–15).

Or why not call this yet another operation of bodies in writing, another curve in language that follows the contours of specific bodies? In a fascinating essay on "The Queen's Throat," also in the volume *Inside/Out*, Wayne Koestenbaum describes exactly this relationship between bodies and institutions and discourses: "The homosexual body, whether silent or vocal, occupies a crossroads where anatomies and institutions collide. Like voice, homosexuality appears to be taking place inside a body, when really it occurs in a sort of outerspace (call it 'discourse') where interiorities converge . . ." (207). It is clear that queer bodies now occupy a conspicuous place in the effort, within numerous discourses but especially in criticism and theory, to return an embodied voice to written critique. In doing so, these bodies call to our attention, often in startling ways, what Butler describes as the continual dialogic exchange between bodies and language, anatomy and imagination: "This is not to say that, on the one hand, the body is simply linguistic stuff or, on the other, that it has no bearing on language. It bears on language all the time. . . . In this sense, then, language and materiality are not opposed, for language both is and refers to that which is material, and what is material never fully escapes from the process by which it is signified" (68).

Following Koestenbaum's metaphor, I would suggest that this continual interchange of language and matter unfolds like a voice, like a space within a body where things converge. I again recall those sites of conjunction described by Elizabeth Grosz: "They are always surface effects between one thing and another—between a hand and a breast, a tongue and a cunt, a mouth and food, a nose and a rose." I hasten to add: word and body, finger and page, tongue and theory.

And they unfold on the surface terrain of writing. Introducing her most recent critical book *Tendencies*, Eve Sedgwick describes her essays as being about "passionate queer things that happen across the lines that divide genders, discourses, and 'perversions,'" not the least of which is the way her own language crosses these lines. As she explains, "I've wanted to recruit—but also where I could, to denude or somehow transfigure—the energies of some received forms of writing that were important to me: the autobiographical narrative, the performance piece, the atrocity story, the polemic, the prose essay that quotes poetry, the obituary" (xiii–xiv). Why not call it all theory? Her essay "A Poem Is Being Written" signals a radical breakdown of discursive boundaries not only because it combines poetry and criticism, or because it fuses autobiographical, personal, and analytical writing, but more so because it builds and turns, crosses, the very boundaries of a fixed sexual body. Not straight but not lesbian, not male but maybe very gay, Sedgwick brings her own undefined, uncategorical body to her writing, "to the epistemological bucking bronco of a more than transsexual identification . . ." (210). What happens to theory when bodily and linguistic categories—male or female, straight or gay—begin to collapse?

Here, I think, is where theory begins to move, within the written word, with all the oral momentum and dynamism characteristic of embodied voices. Sedgwick describes this kind of bodily-linguistic effort: "The expense, rhetorically, of spirit involved, the arduous labor of embodiment required, in 'the finger's–breadth by finger's–breadth' construction of meaning around a site of meaninglessness . . ." (211). This somatic endeavor, "finger's breath by finger's breath," can be a personally and theoretically exhausting undertaking; it can open possibilities even as it disturbs and unsettles. In her essay "White Glasses," Sedgwick moves through the frames of a pair of white glasses belonging to a friend dying of AIDS, and also through her own body as she dons these glasses and confronts the diagnosis of her breast cancer. Here bodies matter all too much, or all too little. What happens when these shifting bodies work their way into theory? The world becomes destabilized, precarious, scary, and at the same time strangely full of possibilities. At one point in "White Glasses," Sedgwick describes the "dizzying array of gender challenges and experiments" that come "with the initiations of surgery, of chemotherapy, of hormone therapy" (263), challenges layered upon the already indecisive identity of one who described herself in the beginning of the essay as "a queer but long-married young woman whose erotic and intellectual life were fiercely transitive . . ." (253). Here is a body, a theory, intensely involved in the "arduous labor" of constructing meaning, putting language to work in all its possible twists and turns. Describing herself after her surgery, Sedgwick writes: "I have never felt less stability in my gender, age, and racial identities, nor, anxious and full of shreds of dread, shame, and mourning as this process is, have I ever felt more of a mind to explore and exploit every possibility" (263–64).

Seizing the possibilities that come from all sorts of shifts and crossings, Sedgwick, as I have noted, embraces the traversals implied in the very etymology of the word "queer." (Alas, the word "lesbian" does not carry within it the momentum of these crossings, though many are the lesbian writers who, as Meese puts it, "intervene in language, reinvent, or better, re-work its texture" [(Sem)Erotics 14].) As Sedgwick explains of such queer theory, "Keenly, it is relational, and strange" (xii).

Yet if Sedgwick's writing is queer, its momentum, its seizing of linguistic opportunities for change and transmutation, connect with the charged surface of much lesbian writing. Alice Parker, for example, writing very self-consciously as a lesbian, describes her work this way: "But when I speak/write as a lesbian the (gendered) center no longer holds. The fact that I speak in the place of the Other problematizes the authorizing discourses that would like to keep me at the margins, or, indeed, invisible" (322). Subjectivities and categories merge, cross, enfold—and all through the continual enfolding of bodies and language. In Parker's writing, as in the writing of other lesbian critics and theorists, theory bends toward poetry: "I study locations: letters, words fly off in all directions, relieved of gravity, sentences turn in/side out. . . . I am sentenced to begin again, unwrite, re-write. Under the covers are certain *sign*als: an in/tensity of the eyes, configurations of the hands. . . . Negotiations (re-claimed from the crass world of commerce): from one language to another(s) and back, transactions, texts juxta-posed, sometimes just brushing against each other, a slight pressure of the fingers. How do you line up tongues?" (324).

Parker embraces the term "polymorphous lesbian body" to seize what she calls a "process metaphor" that is both "indeterminate and precise" (339), that could account for both the specificity and fluidity of lesbian writing. These same kinds of claims, again echoing Sedgwick's notion of the queer, find expression in Judith Roof's book *A Lure of Knowledge: Lesbian Sexuality and Theory*, in which she theorizes lesbian sexuality in terms of "polymorphous diversity." Here lesbian theory embraces its excesses, in bodies and language. As Roof explains, "Adopting a desire for desire instead of a desire for identity or stability may enable a lesbian theory and criticism that really do exceed the singular, the patriarchal, the category lesbian, deploying the lure of knowledge beyond certainty, identity, and mastery" (254). Theory on the move. Knowledge that does not rest with a fixed meaning, but keeps curving with the force of desire.

Something about this lure, this desire, flows from the language of theory. In a pivotal chapter on language, "Beginning With L," Roof follows the lure of Olga Broumas's poem "Beginning With O" in some ways that are similar to my own writing and project. Clearly we are both responding to the lure of Broumas's language, the lure of the O. Yet while I find myself drawn to Broumas's "cave of sound," the oral and aural dimensions of the O, Roof seems enticed by the O of origin, an idea of origins that appears to take us back to a beginning but remains "unlocatable." For her, the O configures lesbian sexuality and language: "The source of writing is evasive and circular like the 'O,' empty and full, beginning, end, middle, playing the paradox of the body as the source of the writing . . ." (129). For me, the O is not evasive, but thick with meanings; the very language of Broumas's poem is not paradoxical, but positively excessive. I read her poetically, listening for the power of poetry to evoke the resonances, the reverberating meanings, of the written word. For Roof, a key word in Broumas's poem is "transliteration," what she describes as translation and transmutation, "the desire to write over, a tracing that simultaneously moves through the past and the future" (139). For me, this "transliteration" happens through the vital sounds of language that Roof herself tries to theorize, to shape into the contours of lesbian sexuality and theory.

Just as Roof reads the O in Broumas's poem in terms of the lure of origins, so I read it in terms of the lure of sounding, audible articulations. Each, in different ways, can urge us on to something else, something more—in language and in knowledge. In this sense, the O becomes a compelling force of desire in language, of a kind described by Julia Kristeva when she speaks of "a passion for ventures with meaning and its materials . . ." (*Desire*, x). When the O lures theory and knowledge, critical traditions are altered from vast repositories of information into remarkably mobile bodies of knowledge—bodies with a desire to maneuver, to curve, to indulge the sensuous lures of language that feed its very existence.

Attempting to theorize such desire in lesbian language and sexuality turns out to be a particularly mobile task, for it always seems to require redefinitions and reconfigurations of theory. And those reconfigurations, it seems to me, are always circling around the O. Even in Teresa de Lauretis's recent book *The Practice of Love: Lesbian Sexuality and Perverse Desire*, a book dense in its analytical rereadings of psychoanalytical theory, the sheer desire that fuels language keeps expanding the contours of de Lauretis's theory of lesbian sexuality. And that is exactly her argument: lesbian sexuality and desire are no longer attached to the phallus, "but able to move on to other images and objects" that can serve as signs for the female body and continually sustain desire itself (223, 243). de Lauretis explains: "For this reason, I would argue, the lesbian subject's desire is 'limitless': in a repeated process of displacement and reinvestment, her desire is a movement toward objects that can conjure up what was never there, and therefore cannot be refound but only found or, as it were, found again for the first time [in Rich's words] ('But in fact we were always like this, / rootless, dismembered: knowing it makes the difference')" (251).

How does this continual, limitless curving of desire work its way into the language of theory, into the language of a book that sets out to theorize lesbian desire? While de Lauretis's writing is dense with the subject and process of analysis, she regards her writing as a the pursuit of "my own passionate fiction through a theoretical fantasy" (85n3), writing that engages the very lesbian desire she theorizes. Near the end of her book, she writes: "That my own critical practice of subjective, dialogic engagement with the texts I cite is itself a practice of love and the exposure of a passionate fiction, should be by now quite apparent: it is only by generic and rhetorical conventions that this book does not read like an autobiography" (293). I can certainly understand how a theorist might engage a "critical practice" that is also a "practice of love," one that is passionately aroused by a "subjective, dialogic engagement" with the texts she reads. I would only add that an ardor for this kind of writing, for theory that is itself driven by desire, also follows the desirous contours of what Broumas calls a "curviform alphabet" that moves along the body and has its source in a "cave of sound." In this curving motion, we may trace the most intense synergy of anatomy and language.

The Crocus

There is another O. It takes its place as part of the continual interworkings of body and language, matter and imagination, through which both bodies and writing incessantly enfold. In her fascinating essay "Critical Clitoridectomy," Paula Bennett speculates about the imagistic significations of the clitoris. Why, she wonders, has feminist theory virtually ignored this particular part of the female anatomy even as it has made the female body a subject of such critical importance? Arguing that we need to turn away from Freudian and Lacanian psychoanalytic models that privilege the phallus and associate women with lack, Bennett explores what she calls a clitoral "symbology," the representation of female sexuality through "small but precious objects" such as buds and berries and jewels. Focusing her attention especially on nineteenth-century American women's writing where these symbols proliferate, Bennett is also interested in the wider implications of clitoral symbology in feminist theory. Of course she is interested as a scholar, but also as a lesbian scholar who, as she explains at the beginning of her essay, shied away from addressing the subject of the clitoris in her academic writing for years, and only now feels confident to discuss openly its "theoretical relevance" in feminist scholarship (236–37).

Among the texts that Bennett turns to is a passage from Virginia Woolf's *Mrs. Dalloway*, one that had already been the subject of Judith Roof's inquiry into lesbian sexuality, and that has subsequently informed Teresa de Lauretis's study of lesbian sexuality and desire. Cited by all three of these critics, I think Woolf's passage is worth quoting fully here, this time for a slightly different reading within the contexts of lesbian theory:

> She could see what she lacked. It was not beauty; it was not mind. It was something central which permeated; something warm which broke up surfaces and rippled the cold contact of man and woman, or of women together. For *that* she could dimly perceive. She resented it, had a scruple picked up Heaven knows where, or, as she felt, sent by Nature (who is invariably wise); yet she could not resist sometimes yielding to the charm of a woman, not a girl, of a woman confessing, as to her they often did, some scrape, some folly. And whether it was pity, or their beauty, or that she was older; or some accident—like a faint scent, or a violin next door (so strange is the power of sounds at certain moments), she did undoubtedly then feel what men felt. Only for a moment; but it was enough. It was a sudden revelation . . . an illumination; a tinge like a blush which one tried to check and then, as it spread, one yielded to its expansion, and rushed to the farthest verge and there quivered and felt the world come closer, swollen with some astonishing significance, some pressure of rapture, which split its thin skin and gushed and poured with an extraordinary alleviation over the cracks and sores! Then for that moment, she had seen an illumination; a match burning in a crocus; an inner meaning almost expressed. But the close withdrew; the hard softened. It was over—the moment. (46–47)

Clitoral symbology? And perhaps *critical* symbology? Woolf's reflections are intensely embodied, but are they also theoretical? Let me turn to another passage from Woolf that Rachael DuPlessis calls to our attention, this one concerning Woolf's own *critical* writing:

> I wish I could invent a new critical method—something swifter and lighter and more colloquial and yet intense: more to the point and less composed: more fluid and following the flight. . . . The old problem: how to keep the flight of the mind, yet be exact. (*Writer's Diary* 324, *Pink Guitar* 60)

What I sense in both of these passages is the experience of and desire for a precise, gemlike kind of sensation—one that Woolf, through Clarissa Dalloway, describes in her body, and that Woolf, as critic, seeks in her language. Something which "breaks up surfaces," something like a "faint scent," or like "the power of sounds at certain moments," something that "spreads" and "expands," something that burns inside: an "inner meaning." Something "swifter and lighter," yet "intense," "fluid," "following the flight," and yet, "exact." Clitoral? Well, why not? The interworkings of body and language, bodily matter and bodily metaphor, are rampant throughout feminist theory, and it does not surprise me that (at least) three feminist theorists should find Woolf's text infused with this particular bodily symbology.

What I would add to readings of this symbology is that this same kind of sensation, let's call it a clitoral sensation, can drive theory as well as fiction. In fact much of the feminist theory I have been discussing is urged on by this very desire for an embodied language that communicates through sound and sensation, in its spreading and copious and expansive dimensions, in its sheer intensity of expression. But in particular (to be "exact"), I would especially call attention to the inner dimensions of this language as it unfolds and yet at the same time remains enveloped within an interior sphere, within what Roof calls its "wrapping," the "petals of the crocus" ("The Match" 252). Although Bennett wants to make the clitoris "visible" and give it representational status, she, too, emphasizes the "self-contained sexuality" and "the "power of inwardly felt and directed desire" that it metaphorizes (246, 248). These same interior dimensions of sensation and language shape the contours of Irigaray's writing, where sound and touch, rather than vision, serve as conduits of language. She imagines "two lips" that are "continually interchanging," a visual image, to be sure, but an image that conjoins voice and kinesis, a metaphor of sounding language. I am reminded of Wittig's image of the fractured j/e, at once seen on the page and yet "spread[ing] itself in the whole world of the book," rebounding and resounding. But whatever the symbology, something about this language "spreads" from within even while it remains "exact" in its very powers of expression. Something about it is remarkably "fluid," and yet singularly "intense." I think not simply of the intensity of spoken language, but specifically how speech becomes all the more intense through bodies, through gesture and breath and vocalization. I think of how such language is remarkably "copious" (in the sense of full bodily feeling, but also in the sense that Walter Ong describes the fullness of oral language)—how it spreads out and "follows the flight" even as it intensely concentrates on an "exact" subject. And I think back to Audre Lorde's essay on the "Uses of the Erotic." In one passage, she describes its powers through a metaphor that might well be part of the clitoral symbology that Bennett explores:

During World War II, we bought sealed plastic packets of white, uncolored margarine, with a tiny, intense pellet of yellow coloring perched like a topaz just inside the clear skin of the bag. We would leave the margarine out for a while to soften, and then we would pinch the little pellet to break it inside the bag, releasing the rich yellowness into the soft pale mass of margarine. Then taking it carefully between our fingers, we would knead it carefully back and forth, over and over, until the color had spread throughout the whole pound bag of margarine, coloring it. (57)

The same kinds of expansion and release within an enveloped interior, the same intensity of sensation, here shape the contours of "erotic knowledge," that fusion of body and intellect so vital in Lorde's writing. Spoken, sounding language unfolds in this fusion, bringing together fingers and thoughts and words.

Just as oral recitations often move in syncopation with fingers manipulating stringed beads (Ong 67), so touch can permeate writing. Gloria Anzaldúa, crossing through multiple identities in her "mestiza" writing, not the least of which is "queer," puts it this way: "I look at my fingers, my feathers, black and red ink drips across the page. *Escribo con la tinta de mi sangre.* I write in red. Ink. Intimately knowing the smooth touch of paper, its speechlessness before I spill myself on the insides of trees" (*Borderlands* 71). This merging of bodies and language, finger touching page, the oral syncopation of finger and word, is what makes possible theories shaped by lips and fingers and, yes, the clitoris. As Broumas would say, it "eases the mind along / the slopes / of the faithful body. . . ." It eases the body into writing, into theory. And it can ease into language even the most interior, and most intense, bodily sensations.

If feminist theory calls forth the female body in writing, then lesbian and queer theory evoke those specific bodily sites where we can seize the intensity of sound and sensation in writing—lips in continual interchange, fingers that work through language, and not least, a clitoral exactness that burns like a match inside a crocus. So exact, in fact, that feminist critics have argued, as only critics might, about the exact configurations of the crocus. For Bennett, the crocus is the clitoris itself, made visible and representable in a symbology directly expressive of female sexuality. For Roof, the crocus is more of a double phallus in its shape, resisting representation in the phallic register, evoking a kind of "representational impossibility." My favorite interpretation is contained in one of de Lauretis's footnotes, in which she describes—in the remarkably situated language of spoken exchange, in its personal and intimate contours, in its grounding in the sheer matter of things—her own experience with crocuses:

> As I am writing this, in the city of Amsterdam and during the week of late-winter school recess that the Dutch call *krokus vakantie* (crocus vacation), I must confess that I actually went for a walk to look at the crocuses, now beginning to bloom in virtually every available bit of soil. This field research proved to me and my companion that both Roof's and Bennett's readings of the image are supported by the shape of the crocus, depending on its stage of bloom. (237n18)

Compared to the larger theoretical terrain of the book, this footnote is, well, a small thing—a bit of a gem. It grounds theory in vision, and yet such sensual vision, almost tactile. Somehow this language evokes just what de Lauretis considers her writing to be: "a critical practice of subjective, dialogic engagement," the "exposure of a passionate fiction" that might read "like an autobiography." Theory as engagement—taking flight, yet exact: a conversation about crocuses.

I return to Elizabeth Grosz and her suggestions of how lesbian desire might *do* something, how it might, let us say, take flight: "They are always surface effects between one thing and another—between a hand and a breast, a tongue and a cunt, a mouth and food, a nose and a rose" (78). If this kind of desire can evoke thought, then its medium in theory is language—an intense and precise critical language carried through sound, curving along bodies and texts.

5

Poetic Literacy

Poetic expression rarely finds a home in the stalwarts of critical writing. As social scientific discourse expands its claim on disciplinary knowledge, so does its increasingly calculating prose. And in the fast-paced, increasingly bureaucratic world of academia, in which the humanities continue to play out a diminishing role, the most prized scholarly writing strips words of their potentially ambiguous turns and holds tight their meandering metaphoric significations.

Poetic / Literacy. That is, written language filled with and fueled by the rhythms, pulsations, and sounds of poetry—and all the distinctive meanings these sounds carry. What could it mean to infuse poetic expression into prosaic critical thought? What might such poetic literacy sound like, signify?

In this final chapter, I would like to bring these questions to feminist theory, and through and beyond that, to an inquiry into the shapings and dimensions and effects of poetic writing in the critical registers of thought. What any culture comes to value as its shared body of knowledge will always unfold through a shared body of language—what E. D. Hirsch calls the "national language" in his book *Cultural Literacy*. I'd like to begin my inquiry into the disposition of this language with a detour through some of Hirsch's ideas, which provoke me to question assumptions about what and how we know—as individuals, and as a culture.

In particular, I'd like to reflect on a passage from *Cultural Literacy* in which Hirsch laments our loss of shared cultural information—in this case, the poetic language of Shakespeare that Hirsch invokes as a means to enhance business communication. Hirsch recounts how his father would often refer to a phrase from Shakespeare's *Julius Caesar* to communicate "complex messages" to his business associates about the "timing of sales and purchases." His father would write, "There is a tide," alluding to the Shakespearean "There is a tide in the affairs of men / Which taken at the flood leads on to fortune," thus urging his associates appropriately to buy or sell now. Although the explanation Hirsch offers centers on his father, let us set aside for the moment this paternal quality of the story, and focus instead on what Hirsch identifies as the moral of this account: it is not that reading Shakespeare will necessarily secure business success, but that today "middle-level executives no longer share literate background knowledge" and that this failure "is a chief cause of their inability to communicate effectively" (9–10).

To be honest, I find myself in some agreement with Hirsch, though I have long abandoned any concern for business communi-cation after years of teaching mindless memo-centered courses in "Effective Business Writing." If only I could have required Shakespeare as a text, or better yet, Emily Dickinson's meticulous economy of language. But more to the point here, I find myself wondering which texts any of us might cite from the records of cultural literacy—which bits of information relayed through rhythmic, alliterative language might carry certain messages and meanings. Let us imagine a mother citing the gnostic gospels: "I am the honored one and the scorned one. / I am the whore and the holy one. / I am the wife and the virgin" (*Gnostic Gospels* xvi). Not a bad set of lines for a woman who wants to establish her authority, or force her interlocutor to engage paradox, or perhaps deal with a snippy business executive. My point is not that the gnostic gospels are any more or less effective than Shakespeare in storing knowledge and enhancing communication. Both constitute for me expressions of poetic literacy, a language that carries through its very sounds and rhythms the message, the idea, the thought.

And both, as Hirsch rightly suggests about the Shakespearean passage, enhance communication. But while Hirsch focuses on the utility of the message—buy or sell now, I would call attention instead to the language—the way sound connects with meaning, facilitating memory and enhancing dialogue. After all, it is not as if Shakespeare's message is devoid of the language that evokes it. We can feel the rhythms of the tide in the alliterative flow from "*af*fairs" to "*f*lood" to "*f*ortune." We can sense it as well in the pacing of each half line of blank verse, in the rhythmic syntactic sequencing of the sentence. In other words, we follow the movements of this tide *in* the poetic language, which in turn shapes the sentence, the message. Something similar happens in the passage I cited from the gnostic gospels. The paradox of "I am the whore and the holy one" is embedded in the very rhythm of the line, its juxtaposed elements, its contrast of conjuncted sounds with "*wh*ore" and "*h*oly." Sounds infuse the written word. These passages do not simply record a message, but shape its very expression.

Such language is not simply a message, devoid of sound and rhythm, and it is not simply some lyrical or ornamental phrase, devoid of meaning. To recall Audre Lorde's words, poetic expression is hardly a "luxury," but rather bears the vital task of connecting language and thought: "Poetry is the way we help give name to the nameless so it can be thought" (37). When I earlier discussed the rhythmic, embodied prose characteristic of many feminist critics and theorists, I recalled Eric Havelock's arguments about the dynamism, fluidity, and concreteness of Greek thought before the institution of alphabetic writing and philosophical abstraction. This kind of poetic language does not simply die out with the onslaught of literacy—as Havelock shows in the transition from orality to literacy in ancient Greece. It maintains itself in certain registers of language and thought, though remaining largely sequestered from the philosophical, intellectual, critical discourses.

But what might happen if this language were not sequestered—if oral, poetic rhythms infused and informed the most valued intellectual discourses within literate traditions? I am not talking about how a familiarity with Shakespeare stands to enhance business communication. I am talking about the very business of communication—speech and writing—to evoke the most powerful resonances of language, to bring them to thought. No small challenge, since the fact remains that we do not produce our valued intellectual texts through poetic language. And we do not read them poetically, or even with reference to poetry.

For the critical registers of intellectual prose, we reserve the qualities of precision, clarity, definition, consistency, abstraction—as if these *alone* promise to enhance knowledge. And as a result, we have for the most part lost an ability to think through complexity and ambiguity, the thick and overlapping meanings of language. Evidence of this loss in American culture is everywhere—from simplistic advertisements to mundane films, from reductive political rhetoric to empirical philosophy to the static, measured language of scientific experimentation. No wonder Shakespeare is invoked in the cause of precise business communication. No wonder the language and thought of science must wrestle with theories of chaos and complementarity, as if more than one meaning must not be ascribed to the complex functionings of chemical and biological phenomena—from quarks and atoms to homonids, genes, the flow of water, the wavelike and bouncing movements of light.

Seizing the poetic dimensions of language and all that it represents is not simply a process of ornamenting language or indulging lyrical expression. It means thinking differently through language, through sounds and rhythms that buzz, thickly, with messages. I call this poetic literacy—the fusing together of oral sounds and literate delineation. Yet this fusion is not produced simply by any fusion of sound and idea, rhythm and theory. And the unfolding of such a literacy within feminist critical writing is not simple to chart.

As I have read and reread a wide range of feminist writing that celebrates and engages such poetic qualities as lyrical expression, metaphoric description, embodied rhythms, personal voice, I find myself discriminating more and more about those writings that are actually able to seize and sustain the tenuous mixture of sound and meaning. Our relative successes and failures should be the subject of lively debate, and in this spirit I turn to several feminist critical writers whose language, and attention to language, has moved me to consider the crucial importance of developing poetic literacy.

In one recent study—itself written in critical, personal, and poetic language—Diane Freedman identifies what she calls "Cross-Genre Writing" among a group of "American feminist poet-critics." Freedman argues that certain hybrid forms of writing signal a distinctive feminist reaction to the confines of purely critical and especially academic discourse. She builds her arguments on many of the expressed frustrations of feminist writers with hierarchical, distanced, patriarchal language, and shows how they have turned, as she has, to more intimate, personal, conversational, poetic modes of writing. And she suggests throughout, along with many of the writers she studies, that such writing strategies are linked to the experiences of women—the intimate and personal lives we lead, the silences and oppression many of us have experienced, perhaps even our "different ways of knowing" that account for a "reliance on narrative, testimony, anecdote, poetry" (14–15).

While I sometimes find myself in agreement with Freedman, I have grown more than a little uneasy with the kind of feminist narrative that underlies her study: conventional academic writing is restrictive and bad, while feminist writing or the "feminine mode" in writing is more connective, opening, liberatory. With Freedman, I want to claim that certain feminist writers have indeed seized and brought to life vibrant forms of writing. But for me, this writing is not necessarily a lyrical celebration of breaking loose from patriarchal discourse by way of engaging personal voice and poetic expression. Nor does it signal an unproblematic "communion with other women as they persist in writing against their absence, silence, and invisibility" (104). Poetic expression complicates literacy, stirs it up—and not necessarily in liberatory ways. In other words, to infuse the rhythms and sounds of poetic language into critical (or cultural) literacy is no more a guarantee of feminist connection than it is of effective business communication.

What then can poetic expression churn up in the critical traditions of literacy? How might its sounding language work to enhance, complicate, enervate modes of intellectual writing that follow a single linguistic path toward definition, clarity, "truth"? Adrienne Rich lays important groundwork for understanding not only how language can work for and among women, but how poetic language is deeply connected to cultural politics—within and beyond feminism. In her most recent book of essays, *What Is Found There: Notebooks on Poetry and Politics*, she describes the signifying power of poetic language, and laments the ways in which these powers are kept outside of, separated from, nonpoetic discourses such as politics and science. She argues that we desperately need the connective forces of metaphor and sound and the "multiple, many-layered, rather than singular, meanings" that they evoke:

> This impulse to enter, with other humans, through language, into the order and disorder of the world, is poetic at its root as surely as it is political at its root. Poetry and politics both have to do with description and with power. And so, of course, does science. We might hope to find the three activities—poetry, science, politics—triangulated, with extraordinary electrical exchanges moving from each to each and through our lives. Instead, over centuries, they have become separated—poetry from politics, poetic naming from scientific naming, an ostensibly 'neutral' science from political questions, 'rational' science from lyrical poetry. . . . (6–7)

Although Rich's readings throughout her book focus directly on poems, on the political implications and meanings carried through the language of poetry, I think her insights bear equally strongly on poetic language that is expressed and written outside the forms of poetry. In other words, just as her arguments call attention to the political meanings of poems, so they are also about the potential poetic signification of a whole variety of discourses. For me, poetic literacy is at the heart of these connections—literate traditions informed by poetic sounds, and poetry itself informed by intellectual traditions and possibilities.

Rich seizes these connections, I think, not only in her readings of poems, but in the meticulous attention she pays to poetic language. At one point, she describes the ability of poetry to sustain memory and story, to encode history. Without it, we lose our material and sensuous connection to the past; we experience what Rich calls a "leak in history." Listen to her describe the distinctly vocal, oral qualities that are lost when poetic language fades away:

The loss can be a leak in history or a shrinking in the vitality of everyday life. Fewer and fewer people in this country entertain each other with verbal games, recitations, charades, singing, playing on instruments, doing anything as amateurs—people who are good at something because they enjoy it. To be good at talk, not pompously eloquent or didactic, but having a vivid tongue, savoring turns of phrase—to sing on key and know many songs by heart—to play fiddle, banjo, mandolin, flute, accordion, harmonica—to write long letters. . . . (79)

In some curious ways, Rich actually sounds like Hirsch when he invokes those lines from Shakespeare as a means of sustaining cultural literacy. Rich, too, recalls the way her father, and her mother, would recite poetry from memory—recitations, she explains, which let us "feel that poetry (verse, really, with its structured rhymes, meters, and ringingly fulfilled aural expectations) was not just words on the page, but could live in people's minds for decades, to be summoned up with relish and verve, and that poetry is not just literature, but embodied voices" (80–81).

Yet for Rich, this poetic language and all its "aural expectations" hardly inform some tradition of cultural literacy of the kind Hirsch recommends. She calls instead on the sounding reverberations of rhythm, meter, voice. As she explains later, "There is a different kind of performance at the heart of the renascence of poetry as an oral art—the art of the griot, performed in alliance with music and dance, to evoke and catalyze a community or communities against passivity and victimization, to recall people to their spiritual and historic sources" (86). These are rhythms and meanings communicated through sound, and through the way that sound can be channeled in written words—the resonances of O as they permeate writing. Rich delineates and brings to life both of these oral and literate movements when she describes the process: "Someone is writing a poem. Words are being set down in a forcefield. . . . Part of the movement among the words belongs to sound—the guttural, the liquid, the choppy, the drawn-out, the breathy, the visceral, the down-light. . . . And in part the field is charged by the way images swim into the brain *through written language*: swan, kettle, icicle, ashes, scab, tamarack, tractor, veil, slime, teeth, freckle" (86–87, italics mine).

Rich's book is an impassioned plea to understand and seize the powers of poetic language, to return to poetry as an instrument—a vocal medium—of political discourse. At the same time, her own poetic writing in *What Is Found There* and throughout her critical essays is an impassioned and embodied enactment of poetic language within the critical registers of literacy. *What* she writes in this book, as well as *how* she writes it, how she activates meaning in language, strikes me as itself a powerful conjunction of poetry and criticism—the sounding energies of poetic language fusing with the intellectual vigor of critical thought. In this passage, where she describes a poetry reading, the poetic and critical take flight together. I'd like to imagine such synergy also informing a philosophical tract, or scientific report, or legal opinion, or critical essay:

> It's an exchange of electrical currents through language—that daily, mundane, abused, and ill-prize medium, that instrument of deception and revelation, that material thing, that knife, rag, boat, spoon-reed become pipe/tree trunk become drum/mud become clay flute/conch shell become summons to freedom/old trousers and petticoats become iconography in appliqué/rubber bands stretched around a box become lyre. . . . Take that old, material utensil, language, found all about you, blank with familiarity, smeared with daily use, and make it into something that means more than it says. What poetry is made of is so old, so familiar, that it's easy to forget that it's not just the words, but poly-rhythmic sounds, speech in its first endeavors . . . prismatic meanings lit by each others' light, stained by each others' shadows. (83–84)

Describing these sounds, these "prismatic meanings," and seizing them in her own critical writing—this is what I have in mind when I speak of poetic literacy. It is a need to bring the powers of poetic language into critical traditions—the discourses of history, science, politics, law, theory, religion, philosophy, letters, and yes, even business memos, memoirs, medicine, the crucial meanderings of language and meaning. It's the "exchange of electrical currents through language," the conjunctive power of sound, that many writers have snuffed out of traditions of cultural literacy. Rich wants us to understand how poetry fosters this crucial political exchange. I think we also need to concern ourselves with how these oral powers of poetic language can and should be brought to literate traditions other than those in the now sequestered domains of poetry and fiction, verse and narrative. Other-wise our literate traditions are defined, isolated, cut off from one another—and so are the peculiar powers of language that fuel discourse within, but rarely beyond, these encampments.

ⓖ

Even enjambment itself . . . worked, in actual poems, not through the
Kristevan semiotic but quite the opposite, through whatever was most
abstract and cognitively under control in the poem, through the forward-
looking and distributive pressure of the syntactic. With that abstraction I
learned to identify.

—(Sedgwick, *Tendencies* 186)

Within feminism, a diverse group of critics and theorists write
poetically—deliberately and conspicuously. I have already discussed
some of these writers in different chapters and contexts—Hélène
Cixous's lyrical criticism, Susan Griffin's poetic essays, Luce Irigaray's
interior alphabet of sound, Elizabeth Meese's erotic prose and letters,
Gloria Anzaldúa's mestiza language, Elizabeth Grosz's desirous
writing, the poetic cadences of Trinh Minh-ha's and Patricia Williams's
critical narratives, and of course Rich's own poetic critiques of and
musings about poetry. And, in slightly different registers, I would add
to this list the kind of lively critical prose that bounces and darts across
the page—the rhetorical flair of Donna Haraway's analysis, the deliberate writerly engagements of Eve Sedgwick. As dissimilar as all these
writings are, they share a self-conscious attempt to merge sound and
thought, ear and epistemology.

But why would so many feminist thinkers—as a heterogeneous
yet conspicuous group—make this turn in language toward a poetic
literacy? As I have mentioned earlier, I'm both respectful and distrustful
of certain suggestions, such as those made by Freedman and others,
that feminist poetic modes of criticism are distinctly connected to
women's experiences, particularly to the silences and invisibility
women have experienced within traditions of writing. Just because
women have been silenced—and they emphatically have been, in many
ways—does not necessarily mean that they, or that feminist critics, will
write poetically, any more than they might write abstractly, formally,
objectively. The choice to engage poetic modes of thought, to make
poetic language a vital part of criticism, is just that—a choice—
deliberate, calculated, and carefully embraced. To claim that feminists
write poetically because poetry is somehow a more "feminine mode" of
language, or may reflect "women's ways of knowing," or may provide
emotional comfort and "communion" among women, is to situate
poetry, like orality, as the other side of a masculine literacy. Yet poetic
language, as I have also emphasized earlier, is not simply some refuge
from the literate traditions of men. Far from that, it stirs up, complicates
literacy—makes it at once clear and convoluted, precise and ambiguous,

abstract and sensuous. It helps us create and remember complex thoughts through sound. Linking rhythm and message, poetry—like both oral language and distinctly sensory modes of writing—can sustain memory, history, cultural traditions, things we want to know, ponder, reconsider, confirm, change.

I believe that many feminist thinkers have turned to poetic language so that they can engage this particularly intense process of knowing. Or, to put it differently, I think that poetic literacy intensifies and expands the very domains of epistemology, critique, theory. Feminist critics are not running away from dominant modes of writing that have shunned emotion, intimacy, dialogue. Instead, they are stirring them up within literacy, mixing and complicating their different sounds and meanings.

That these disruptions should emerge through a distinctly *sounded* writing—abundant in its oral and aural dimensions—indicates that some pivotal turns are altering the tenor and signification of critical thought. We know that poetic rhythms and sounds have the ability to jar us deeply, just as they can lull and comfort on different occasions. Within the critical registers of writing, they have a special ability to shake things up significantly, often shockingly. They can critique staid traditions of thought through resounding and vibrating messages, making sound a component of thought. I often recall my own initial shock at reading the lyrical outbursts of Cixous, for example: "But look, our seas are what we make of them, full of fish or not, opaque or transparent, red or black, high or smooth, narrow or bankless; and we are ourselves sea, sand, coral, seaweed, beaches, tides, swimmers, children, waves . . . More or less wavily sea, earth, sky—what matter would rebuff us? We know how to speak them all" (260).

As a literary critic accustomed to the conventions of critical writing, I simply was not prepared for this kind of description of language, or prepared to understand how we might read and "speak" such language. I found myself searching through the text for some explanatory statement, some summary comments that would bring it all together. But of course the meanings here are not found in summary statements about this or that; they resonate through the very sounds of the words that exemplify and take us toward a different conception of writing and thinking. I recall one student who was initially extremely frustrated with Cixous's writing, later informing me that when she began to read Cixous out loud, everything made sense. It hit me that the significance of Cixous's writing was in its appeal to the senses—the way in which its "oral phonetic" quality, as Cixous describes her own language, engages the ear, forces the eye to make way for sound and its tactile dimensions, the breath and vibrations of voice. Sound becomes a palpable force in reshaping written word, altering epistemology.

In an essay that is not itself expressly poetic, but does make claims for personal and poetic voice in criticism, Jane Tompkins provides an apt example of how a poetic word—its very sound—can both critique and reshape epistemology. In "Me and My Shadow," Tompkins quotes a sentence from Ellen Messer Davidow about feminist epistemology: "'In time we can build a synchronous account of our subject matters as we glissade among them and turn upon ourselves.'" Reflecting on this statement, Tompkins writes: "What attracted me to the sentence was the 'glissade.' Fluidity, flexibility, versatility, mobility" (127–28).

I agree. The word "glissade" makes me slow down and *think*— think about our possible movements and potential versatility within feminism, and further, become rather upset, often sad, when such versatility gives way to stiff pronouncements about this or that. I also think about the imperative to glide through thought; I mean the way it is sometimes absolutely necessary to let yourself go, let yourself fall back into and within complex theories and ideas. In the word "glissade" I find the expressed, sounded powers of poetic literacy. I am not insisting that we could or should always engage such smooth intellectual reflection, but that, at least in this case, critical literacy must make room for both the rigors and relaxation of language. "Glissade" is not simply a poetic term. More important, it evokes—through sound and meaning—a way to think, reflect, consider and reconsider, the possible turns of ourselves and our thinking.

As it turns out, Tompkins is in fact writing about epistemology— critiquing certain feminist ideas about what constitutes epistemology, and then running away from the very distancing language she herself uses in her critique. She tires of her own "watered-down expository prose," and laments the loss of poetry in her writing:

> Not much imagery. No description of concrete things. Only that one word, 'glissade.'
>
> > Like black swallows swooping and gliding
> > in a flurry of entangled loops and curves . . .
>
> Two lines of a poem I memorized in high school are what the word 'glissade' called to mind. Turning upon ourselves. Turning, weaving, bending, unbending, moving in loops and curves. (128)

We are back again with Rich, remembering and thinking through alliterative rhythm. This sounding language does not run away from epistemology; it engages it directly, sensuously, in order to talk about some crucial issues that a more distanced, abstract language cannot communicate—at least not here, not for Tompkins. For a good deal of what Tompkins wants to write about is actually not epistemology, but anger—or more precisely, the ways in which discussions of epistemology make her angry. In one sense, in one tone of voice, she can describe this anger fairly straightforwardly, prosaically, as she explains the kind of anger that she and her colleagues feel at "our exclusion from the discourse of 'Western man' . . . anger is what fuels my engagement with feminist issues; an absolute fury that has never even been tapped, relatively speaking. It's time to talk about this now, because it's so central, at least for me. I hate men for the way they treat women, and pretending that women aren't there is one of the ways I hate most" (136).

This is a remarkably direct statement—clear, precise, forceful, unambiguous. But then, Tompkins becomes less sure about her anger, its sources and directions. The story gets complicated. Is this purely feminist anger? Is it, as she wonders, something "pent up" from her childhood? Reflective of a general problem with authority, with men in authority, with a desire to please and then be angry about pleasing? All this, and more. And with this more complicated reflection, Tompkins turns again to a more poetic language: "The rage I feel inside me now is the distillation of forty-six years. It has had a long time to simmer, to harden, to become adamantine, a black slab that glows in the dark" (137).

The pages of my copy of Tompkins's much reprinted essay are marked with different pens, pencils, two distinct shades of yellow highlighter, showing my own multilayered and differing readings of her writing. I remember her points about and frustrations with epistemology, but have committed to memory the phrases like "watered-down expository prose" (something about the "w"s and "p"s), "glissade" and "simmer" and "black slab" (definitely something about those "s"s). I recall these words, too, through the title, taken from a song, from verse: "Me and my shadow / strollin' down the avenue" (Tompkins says "walkin' down the avenue," but I remember "strollin'"). I have come to think about the potential hisses and buzzings surrounding epistemology through these sounds, through the messages and critiques they evoke.

And like all sounds, they linger. In fact what draws me to Tompkins's essay is that it does not lead to any neat conclusions, certainly to no definitions of epistemology, not even to a firm sense of the role of personal writing in criticism. But it takes us—gliding and simmering—through the process of rethinking these issues. And while

Tompkins does not write poetry, or even a highly poetic prose, I think she occasionally, and very deliberately, engages a ringing poetic language for some of her most important critical reflections. I think that she wants to move away from the kinds of watered-down prose that typically characterize critical writing, that she wants to tap into and follow a sounding language as a way to rethink epistemology.

Then again, there are glissades and there are glissades. I do not want to conflate all poetic expressions within feminist criticism to some massive, singular transformation of thought. Poetic language, after all, has a way of turning on and within itself, carrying thick meanings and messages. As Rich says of poetry, I would say of poetic literacy: its meanings are not "singular," but "multiple" and "multi-layered"—like Tompkins's anger. And for this very reason I have mixed feelings about different modes of poetic criticism that work to enforce singular meanings, even as they critique and break open other dominant singular meanings that should rightly be called into question. Sometimes, I fear, feminists are too eager to claim that personal voice is our source of liberation, or that lyrical reflection will necessarily open for us—or for anyone—new modes of thinking and communicating.

This is where I come back to the risky business of the O. Yes, there are the expressive powers of its curviform, sounding alphabet, its urgent meanings. But what if these powers end up serving another cause, another system of meaning, potentially as restrictive as the one they call into question? Or, what if poetic language does not lead anywhere beyond self-expression and reflection? Of course there are places for, whole traditions of, such writing, and I hardly want to restrict the possibilities for any of the myriad forms of expressive, reflective, lyrical writing. But my own sense of poetic literacy—especially as I see it unfolding within feminist writing—is that it builds on a careful, sometimes tenuous and always risky, engagement with both sound and meaning, both driving oral rhythms and the more settled pace of literate deliberation.

And so I worry when critical writing gets out of whack—literally, out of meaningful rhythm and pace with our ability to think. We already know, on the one hand, the constraints of a critical tradition that makes no room for the sounds and rhythms of language—the "watered-down expository prose" that marks so much calculating philosophy and theory. But, on the other hand, there is also the indulgence in lyrical language that does not necessarily lead to productive ways of thinking through language. As much as I appreciate some of Mary Daly's playful turns of language, for instance, I wonder where the puns and parody take us. In turning her back on language itself as inherently patriarchal, what remains? Where is there, or can there be, a serious engagement with these rhythmic and alliterative twists of words and sounds? Contrasting Rich's and Daly's ideas about language, Jane Hedley notes a marked difference in their linguistic critiques and investments. While both writers harbor a deep distrust of language that seems always to serve the purposes of patriarchy, Daly becomes increasingly exclusive about metaphoric meanings, yet Rich will rework the language we have for all its possibilities: "'This is the oppressor's language / But I need it to talk to you.'"

When Rich says that she needs this language "to talk to you," I am again reminded of the oral, dialogic imperatives of poetic language and literacy. Such sounding prose has a unique ability to move us—to carry and deliver meanings. And this moving force, I believe, is what accounts for Rich's commitment to language, specifically her commitment to its poetic powers: to mix up words, rearrange and reconfigure them so that we might not simply play with, but seriously reconfigure their possible significations. Not parody, but plenitude. Not one continuing critique of patriarchy, but a continuing engagement, through language, that deepens the possibilities of critique.

I think such possibilities also become restricted—get out of whack, so to speak—when poetic language serves too exclusively as a vehicle of lyrical self-expression. Again, not that there is anything wrong with lyrical reflection. But in poetic literacy, I want it to go somewhere, to move with thought. Jeffner Allen, for example, very rightly criticizes the separation of poetry and philosophy. Yet her attempts to carve out a poetic philosophy in her book *reverberations*, for me at least, indulge a long lyrical flow of words that drift away from thought, almost as if they are not anchored in sounded messages and meanings. When Allen describes her writing, for instance—"spacious writing of the r e v e r b e r a t i o n s gathers and dissolves *with nearby* joy sorrow grief compassion *alongside on the edges of* womyn loving womyn longings womyn lovings and womyn storms *across* genocides murders crashes economic deprivations nationalisms ____ and out of this   SEVERALS SURPRISING   a healing   perhaps" (1)—I find myself wanting a less spacious prose, something more condensed and thick with meanings. Instead of a sentence ending with "perhaps" that dissolves into vague possibilities, I want specific articulations that describe and critique this world of grief, loving, genocide, and deprivation. I want, in critical literacy, something like Rich's poetic lines:

> If I could let you know—
> two women together is a work

nothing in civilization has made simple,
two people together is a work
heroic in its ordinariness,
the slow-picked, halting traverse of a pitch
where the fiercest attention becomes routine
—look at the faces of those who have chosen it. (*Dream* 35)

We need to capture in critical writing this fierce attention, these faces, the connections between what is simple and slow-picked, what is heroic and halting in the everyday, ordinary work of life—of language.

To glissade through language may not be the same thing as glissading through thought. And in fairness to Allen, perhaps she is seeking more of a flight from the rigorous language of philosophy. Perhaps this is what she wants of language just now. But what I want of poetic literacy is something different, in this case, more like Rich's actual poem. I believe that in critical and theoretical writing we cannot too easily give over the rigors of thought to a flowing lyricism, any more than we can afford to lose the lyrical powers within intellectual traditions. As I say, the O can be tricky business, tenuous, treacherous, thick with the buzzing of sound and thought.

Nor can we give over the rigors of thought to compact, easy, neat messages about feminism, oppression, patriarchy, or language itself. In some of her remarks on language, bell hooks describes the fullness of the language spoken in the kitchen, where her mother and grandmother and sisters and other "women friends" gathered to talk: "There, black women spoke in a language so rich, so poetic, that it felt to me like being shut off from life, smothered to death if one were not allowed to participate" (5). We might well ponder how such rhythmic, poetic language becomes a vital force in a whole variety of critical and cultural traditions. For this very reason, I am troubled by hooks's deprecation of much feminist theory as "elitist" and "linguistically convoluted" (36), and her calls for an "oppositional discourse, the liberatory voice" that will transform consciousness. As an example of such "linguistically convoluted" theory, hooks turns to some of the writings of Luce Irigaray and Julia Kristeva: "Although this work honors the relationship between feminist discourse and political practice, it is often used within university settings to establish a select intellectual elite and to reinforce and perpetuate systems of domination, most obviously white Western cultural imperialism" (40).

How theory and language are "used within university settings" might well be analyzed as rigorously as how language is used within kitchen settings. But to jump from such analysis to general accusations about imperialism strikes me as hasty indeed. The "world of woman speech" emphatically begs for our critical attention, but it may not be so distant from other worlds where people harbor similar longings for such abundant language—especially within the university setting. We need an invigorated language not to shout out accusations about some conspiracy of the intellectual elite to promote western domination, but to get down to the details—in carefully chosen, thoughtful words, syntax, semantic turns—about such imperative matters as racism, oppression, sexuality, gender, theory, poetry, intimacy, intensity, imperialism. These are all heavy words, heavy concepts. We need the thick meanings and sounds of words to work our way through their complex significations. A language that is not so much thesis-driven, as driven beyond even the important arguments it advances—into areas of questioning, uncertainty, halting reconsideration and caution within its determined, quick momentum.

I believe many feminists have been especially eager to seize this language because we have needed it to reconsider virtually everything—from vast systems of thought to the details of daily exchange. In this sense, and again, especially for feminists, poetic literacy becomes the exact opposite of cultural literacy conceptualized as a shared system of knowledge. Poetic literacy is the language that rebounds within that system, urging us to pay attention—fierce attention—to meanings and significations that exceed its coherence. At times the sheer ability of poetic language to shake up systems of knowledge is its most distinctive feature—as in Susan Griffin's *Woman and Nature: The Roaring Inside Her*. Here Griffin very deliberately assumes a voice that subverts, or as she says, goes "underneath logic . . . by writing associatively . . ." (xv). Her argument is inseparable from her language—and her language, in turn, shapes every reconsideration, every idea. She explains: "Thus my prose in this book is like poetry, and like poetry always begins with feeling" (xv).

In many ways, Griffin's purpose is to feel her way back through a vast system of ideas and representations—coded in the literate traditions of philosophy, history, and science—in which women and nature are equated and mutually consigned to the place of inert matter. But the vehicle for feeling her way back is not a new or different mode of writing. It is language that oozes out of the very texts she contemplates, poetry turning from and into critical prose, unleashing the harnessed energies within these systems of representation. Griffin works language, works with and through language, to question and transform shared systems of knowledge. Not a stabilized language that secures cultural cohesion, but poetic language that unsettles such cultural codings. Luce Irigaray wonders if women's desire might speak itself in a "different alphabet" (*This Sex* 25), perhaps, I have also suggested, one similar to Olga Broumas's "curviform alphabet . . . beginning with O." We can hear the sounds of this lettering in Griffin's writing on "Erosion," where the language of science turns into poetry, where—*through poetic language*—representations of women and nature turn inside out, inert matter takes on life:

> Ablation. Abrasion. Mountain of accumulation. Aeolian
> deposits. Afforestation. *Testimonies. Over and over we*
> *examined what was said of us. Over and over we testify.*
> *The lies. The conspiracy of appearances.* There are
> Fissures. There are cracks in the surface. (194)

She continues, letter by letter, in alphabetic fashion, refashioning words, sounds, and meanings:

> Backwash. Basalt. Basin. Bedrock. Blizzard. Bute. In
> the bath she sees suddenly that her legs are women's
> legs. . . . Calving. (The iceberg detaches from the glacier.)
> Canyon. . . . Jet streams, Key, Lagoon, Lake, Lava, Magma,
> Metamorphosis, Meteor (shooting star). *We can tell you how*
> *words spoken in rage accumulate around us. How we make our*
> *home in this language.*
> Monsoon Forest. Moraine. Nadir. Oasis. Plain. Planet.
> *Suddenly we find we are no longer straining against all the*
> *old conclusions. We are no longer pleading for the right to*
> *speak: we have spoken; space has changed; we are living in*
> *a matrix of our own sounds; our words resonate, by our*
> *echoes we chart a new geography. . . .*
> Quartz, Quagmire, Radiation. Rain. River. Rock.

To be moved again and again to speech, to live in a matrix of sounds. These operations of language, these utterances, force language to crack open beyond its assigned meanings. They mark the places of Griffin's "fissures," "cracks in the surface."

Published in 1978, alongside such powerful feminist manifestos as Cixous's "Laugh of the Medusa" and Rich's *Dream of a Common Language*, Susan Griffin's *Woman and Nature* gave voice to a kind of feminist criticism that emphatically bucked patriarchal language and knowledge. As such, it makes all too generalized claims about women, about women's language, that might well be qualified today, a mere two decades later. Yet as feminist pronouncement, Griffin's is a timely work in the ongoing shaping of feminist critical writing and its distinctly poetic cast. She uses every bit of language—every letter and sound and signification—to critique systems of cultural literacy from within, to speak and write her way through and beyond their cohesive confines. Hers is the O as it roars. Yet this roaring sound is never just pure sound, pure outburst detached from articulation, idea, thought. Griffin wants to discover, through language, what we can know. Not a new idea, but how language can reconfigure ideas, knowledge, reality. *"For we did not invent the blackbird, we say, we only invented her name"* (226).

This statement, from the book's final section on "Matter: How We Know," hardly signals some escape from thought, but the vital reconnection of matter and language—*how* we know. Griffin's work is far from pure poetic reflection. In fact it is filled with fact, packed tight with textual citations that constitute the hallmark of a dominant cultural literacy. Even a passing glance through her copious endnotes and bibliography would provide ample evidence of Griffin's "fierce attention" to a wide array of culturally sanctioned documents ranging from Aristotle and Bacon to Freud, Heisenberg, Whitehead. She reworks and rewords them, takes on systems of knowledge in order to continue to know—

> Because I know I am made from this earth . . . I know this earth, the body of the bird, this pen, this paper, these hands, this tongue speaking, all that I know speaks to me through this earth and I long to tell you, you who are earth too, and listen *as we speak to each other of what we know.* (227)

I am not sure that Griffin comes to any neat conclusions about what we *should* know. Instead, she keeps reminding us that we are connected to a vital earth and language that give us the means to keep reworking what we *can* know. Her own writing works hard to break through a confining literacy. It is not the only path or potential for poetic literacy, but it does mark one of the most conspicuous "cracks in the surface" of literate traditions. And Griffin, I think, wants to stay near that fault line, the place where a sounding language cracks open systems of knowledge. I recall her remarks from her more recent essay *Red Shoes*:

> I love that moment in writing when I know that language falls short. There is something more there. A larger body. Even by the failure of words I begin to detect its dimensions. As I work the

prose, shift the verbs, look for new adjectives, a different rhythm, syntax, something new begins to come to the surface. (8)

That moment where language falls short, where cracks and fissures appear, where erosion sets in—these very words nudge me on to another metaphor: the edge, the jagged edge of a border. Such borders of and within language mark precisely those often jagged lines that demarcate poetry and prose, speech and writing, intimate and official styles, different national languages, cohesive and dialogic and disruptive modes of discourse. When Griffin, for instance, says that she loves the moment when cracks and fissures emerge in language, I'm reminded of the fierce attention so many contemporary theorists have devoted to the potentially generative gaps and omissions within language—places where the circuit of meaning does not come full circle, the clashes, hyphens, the elisions in sentence and signification. As I have argued elsewhere, in an essay on such critical spacings, these cracks and fissures have often served as crucial spaces for many feminist theorists, especially those interested in imprecise borders and fluid boundaries, the complex zones where difference becomes multidimensional rather than simply binary ("Theory and Space"). I recall citing lines from Adrienne Rich's poem that concludes her volume *Your Native Land, Your Life*:

> the body's pain and the pain on the streets
> are not the same   but you can learn
> from the edges that blur   O you who love clear edges
> more than anything   watch the edges that blur (111)

What can it mean to inhabit, to learn from, these edges? How is it that writing across these permeable zones of sound and sense might become potentially transformative for feminist writers, or indeed for anyone? I have turned to the work of Gloria Anzaldúa on several occasions throughout this book, but have wanted to save a fuller discussion of her writing for now—not only because she occupies, for me, a prominent place in the voicing of poetic literacy, but because she has written in such poetic and thoughtful ways about the transformative potential of borders—in language and in life. What's more, Anzaldúa's writings on the emergence of "mestiza" consciousness have helped me contextualize some of my own notions about the boundaries of oral and literate expression, especially the edges that mark where they blur into each other and produce what Anzaldúa calls a "continual creative motion that keeps breaking down the unitary aspect of each new paradigm" (80).

In many ways, Anzaldúa's *Borderlands / La Frontera* is a book about language, even as its principal subject concerns the mixture and collusion of cultures, specifically Chicano/a culture of the Mexican–United States border. Written half in prose, half in poetry, Anzaldúa delves into her own historical, spiritual, and linguistic traditions and the unique kinds of crossings and mixtures that have shaped them. Language plays no small part in this entire endeavor. She describes her own language as "a new language—the language of the Borderlands," a mingling of Castillian Spanish and Nahuatl, English and North Mexican dialect—and, I would add, the languages of poetry, autobiography, narrative, critical analysis, theory. Elsewhere I have described Anzaldúa's feel for the fleshy, sensuous dimensions of her writing, linking them to the tactile dimensions of oral language and to the distinctly embodied modes of language that characterize so much feminist writing. What I want to emphasize now is how this language derives from linguistic borderlands, how it unfolds at the edges where body and mind, poetry and theory, spoken and written word rub up against each other, producing that "continual creative motion" that informs the mestiza consciousness.

The very word consciousness is crucial—a state of awareness, a means of knowing. When Anzaldúa describes what it means to be mixed, hybrid, mestiza, I do not hear her talking about conditions of being, but active processes, ways of thinking that move beyond singular ideas and identities. Describing the mestiza, Anzaldúa writes: "She has discovered that she can't hold concepts or ideas in rigid boundaries. . . . The new *mestiza* copes by developing a tolerance for contradictions, a tolerance for ambiguity" (79). Again I am reminded of Rich's claims about poetry, about the "multiple, many-layered rather than singular meanings" that it communicates. But Anzaldúa is not writing poetry here, at least in this particular essay "La conciencia de la mestiza / Towards a New Consciousness." She is writing a mixed and layered language—English, Spanish, Chicano Spanish; she is writing in mixed modes—analysis, metaphorical description, personal narrative, dialogue, and yes, some poetry. She is writing the "cultural collision" (78) that she invokes.

In her chapter "Tlilli, Tlapalli / The Path of the Red and Black Ink," Anzaldúa explains the specific kinds of mestiza forces that shape her own writing. It is not simply a matter of mixed languages and hybrid writing styles. It is the sheer tumult, the anxiety of thought, unfolding in language. Thus her bold claim: "Living in a state of psychic unrest, in a Borderland, is what makes poets write and artists create" (73). This kind of generative unrest no doubt can have many sources and manifestations, and for me, at least, one of these is the conjunction of sound and meaning, the place where language resonates beyond strict or singular messages, where it becomes unsettled, uneasy. Anzaldúa turns to the red and black ink painted on Aztec codices to explain these mestiza forces in her own writing, describing how these colors symbolized *"escritura y sabiduría* (writing and wisdom)," a conjunction of "poetry and truth" (69). But this is not a staid form of knowledge, some neat path leading to a fixed truth. Again and again, Anzaldúa will speak of confusion and torment and uncertainty: "Writing produces anxiety" (72). Her image is not the controlling pen, but fleshy images of mouth and a "wild tongue":

> To be a mouth—the cost is too high—her whole life enslaved to that devouring mouth. *Todo pasaba por esa boca, el viento, el fuego, los mares y la Tierra.* Her body, a crossroads, a fragile bridge, cannot support the tons of cargo passing through it. She wants to install "stop" and "go" signal lights, instigate a curfew, police Poetry. But something wants to come out. (74)

This fleshy oral passageway for language, and the relentless, heavy cargo of words, messages: Anzaldúa's metaphors make me ponder the extent to which traditions of cultural literacy have in effect already policed poetry, especially those poetic powers of language that keep writing and thought in a state of tumult, anxiety, collision. To what extent has critical writing turned away from poetic language so as to avoid these fissures and all their crucial complications? To what extent have the borderlands within language and signification been policed?

If we are wary, as I am, that poetic language has been policed, then how might we negotiate our way through the tumult and anxieties of language that is brimming with signification? Such a question strikes me as especially crucial for feminist scholars, because we do have very clear, precise, mouthy arguments to advance. I would insist that we need to make poetic literacy work as a critical tool, as theory, as a precise and precocious way of thinking and rethinking. And I believe that this is exactly what many of the sharpest feminist thinkers have accomplished with their poetic prose.

I have saved for last a rather precise example of how this task unfolds—not in some general theory about language, but as a deliberate effort to put poetic language to work in criticism—specifically literary criticism. In a chapter of her book *The Pink Guitar: Writing as Feminist Practice*, Rachael DuPlessis tries to come to terms with the poetry of H.D. and the ambivalent position she occupied in some rather sexist moments of literary modernism. To a large extent, DuPlessis's chapter is biographical, analytical, and critical. But it also reads like poetry. It reads like criticism turned to poetry, like a critical voice turned poetic in order to express the plight of a woman whose life and works require a different kind of critical language. We encounter a mixture, juncture of description and speculation, quotations and reflections. Sometimes DuPlessis sounds rather straightforward, as when she describes H.D.'s relationship with the men of modernism: "At one stage H.D. had to reject these men, in order to survive, and then later she had to remember them, to glory in that male attention, the male sun gleaming and brilliant" (23). I say rather straightforward, because by the end of the sentence we are already moving into poetic language, already breaking through the composed description of "male attention" and into the metaphoric "male sun gleaming and brilliant." We know that H.D. is struggling, struggling to negotiate a position for herself in this decidedly masculine literary circle. Listen to DuPlessis as she writes about this struggle:

> Choice for the woman: be appropriated . . . Or be isolated. So H.D. chooses images of pupae, slugs, worms, snails, the larval bits of undistinguished but fecund matter which crawl and ooze and survive. They seem dumb, dull. Can be overlooked, won't threaten, are negligible. (27)

These poetic images belong to H.D., but they are now also part of DuPlessis's own critical writing, which itself becomes increasingly imagistic, metaphoric, rhythmic—an altogether different language than what we are accustomed to hearing in literary criticism. This same kind of transferral happens with H.D.'s image of the volcano, which becomes for DuPlessis as powerful an image of repression and blockage— "Sexual passion" and "patriarchal structure"—as it seemed for H.D. in her own poetry. Such images weave their way throughout DuPlessis's critical writing, at times describing H.D.'s cultural constraints, at times becoming for DuPlessis a way to work through her own struggles with a confining critical language:

> Insomnia again.

> Rigidity. It makes a surface, impacted and tingling where there was depth. Depth refused, perpetually postponed. Therefore all that possibility, deep corridors of the self and sleep, the elegant tunnelings of dreams erupt silently and maliciously. Harden.

Insomnia, as the refusal of exploration, generates symptoms of
refusal, like the lump in the throat (neck, breaking point). . . . (29)

Should we understand this as a poetic critical assessment of H.D.?
DuPlessis's own critical self-reflection? An attempt to break through the
most rigid of structures—language as volcano? These hard images
continue to appear—in H.D., in DuPlessis: crystals, stones, sphinx.
DuPlessis works through them, infuses their hardness into her own
critical language, makes of criticism a poem, at times, as:

> The woman is pensive, inward, also a block of matter.
> This is "Thought."
> This essay is about a woman, so there is a rock. She is
> looking into hewn block, into stone pool, into the one core
> of earth given for her solid head to come from. To mirror.

Or as in the lines with which DuPlessis concludes this chapter:

> Woman. Rock. Equal halves of the balance pole, joined by
> her
> neck the
> well
> from which a voice may come resisting its power,
> buried to the neck,
> wounded
> in the neck
> born up through the glottal inelegant column. (40)

My questions about DuPlessis's writing on H.D.: Why this turn in
language? Why this sense of something thick, hard, confining, that she
must break through? Is this effort, this language, necessary for the
woman poet, the woman critic? How does this writing constitute
"feminist practice," as DuPlessis describes her writing in the book's
subtitle?

In a final essay, "The Pink Guitar," DuPlessis explains some of the
contours of this practice: "Writing not as personality, writing as praxis.
For writing is a *practice*—a practice in which the author disappears into
a process, into a community, into discontinuities, into a desire for
discovery. . . . shrill, hysterical, sentimental, washing up the dirtying,
obtuse, querulous, unsuccessful, critical, synthetic, ruining . . ." (172).
She then ponders: "I am doing work, and what kind of work is it? for
whom am I working? and what am I bringing into being?" (173). And I

would add: Just what is it that we are practicing? And what are we practicing for? New ways to read poems, and perhaps more?

In some sense, it is not terribly surprising to find a literary critic writing poetically. Others have done it before and after DuPlessis, and as she herself says, "many people have reinvented the essay" (175). But I think something more is happening here—something that, as DuPlessis emphasizes, is peculiarly linked though not restricted to feminist writing, and that also moves well beyond the strict domain of literary criticism. And so to answer one of my questions, are we practicing new ways to read poems, I would respond yes, and in this case especially women's poetry. But we are also practicing and inventing new ways to read and write through the very terms of that poetry—ways to think and criticize through the overlapping powers of poetic and critical language. In terms of the image DuPlessis uses to describe her critical endeavor, we are practicing on the pink guitar, learning to play the pink guitar. Picking it up, she finds "that the languages, the words, the drives, the genres, the keyboards, the frets, the strings, the holes, the sounding boards, the stops, the sonorities have been filled with representations that depend, in their deepest satisfactions, on gender and sexual trajectories that make claims upon me (and could compromise what I do)" (158). And so she has to unlearn, rework the very material of language, "unpick everything," as she says: "It's like the ground of the page. The blankness already filled with words through which one negotiates" (159). This is not inventing some new feminist language. Far from that, it means practicing, reworking, critically negotiating our way through the language we have, the texts we read, the language we use to reread those texts.

The idea of practicing language, like practicing music, itself resonates throughout contemporary theories of language—in feminism and elsewhere. I recall de Certeau's emphasis of "practice" and "enactment" through language, and their connection to the "art of speaking." And more particularly, I recall how Griffin moves through language, rearranging letters, words, meanings; and how Anzaldúa seizes the unsettling potential of mestiza language to keep consciousness in a productive state of unrest. You learn music by practicing it, enacting it—using fingers, vocal chords, rhythm, breath, the vibrations of sound felt on the skin. Can it be so different with language, with thought itself?

And this practice, I believe, is in turn connected to what many theorists mean by "performance": the sheer enactment of language and thought, how we become who we are, how we might resignify and rethink ourselves, our ideas. On this stage, we encounter the workings of poetry and power. Here I recall Judith Butler: "Performative acts are forms of authoritative speech . . . statements that, in the uttering, also perform a certain action and exercise a binding power. . . . If the power of discourse to produce that which it names is linked with the question of performativity, then the performative is one domain in which power acts as discourse" (*Bodies* 225). Within this tangled domain of language and power, words and enactments, feminist theory utters its messages. For DuPlessis, such a practice becomes a musical performance.

It somehow seems right to me that DuPlessis should choose a musical instrument as her metaphor for language, for this reworking and retuning of language and thought. After all, her own critical language is fueled by poetic rhythms. It sounds. It is abundant in its own oral and aural dimensions. And so her writing resonates with more than one meaning, breaking through what she calls "a clean pure lyric line, a clean pure polemical line, a clean pure logic, a real identity, a real origin, the real story . . ." (66). The line is messy, jagged: "I have engaged in some trek through poly-present languages. Heterogeneous and self-questioning, judgmental and polyvalent, craving and craven—this is the practice. The pleasures of a doing, an on-goingness, a finding, a coming-to, a beginning again and again" (66). And again, Broumas: "Beginning with O," but not coming full circle. No wonder that DuPlessis, like Anzaldúa and Irigaray, turns to fleshy, oral images to describe her writing:

> Dream: a cakey red lipstick mouth, pouty and intense
> The lips part
> out of which the protrubering shape of a "form"
> . . . .
> What am I doing? What are these desirous "wounds" these
> great gapings?
>
> What is that big red mouth?   (66–67)

In her early essay "For the Etruscans," DuPlessis plays with the notion that such polyvalent, fleshy writing may represent a distinctive "female aesthetic," a notion that she at times seems to want to embrace, but ultimately runs away from, since any variety of oppositional or subversive writing practices can be seized by any group of people, any individual, for diverse purposes (16). Yet there is no question that the feminist writers who have in fact seized this language have done so for distinctly feminist purposes. In her chapter on poet and critic Susan Howe, DuPlessis keeps reframing the question of why:

Why does Howe erase or elide some words. . . . Why does she
confound grammar? . . . Why does she use syllable-sounds of
semi-meaning? . . . Why and how vibrations of shadow words. . . .
Why does she make pages of cut-ups, of upside-downs, of
palimpsests? Traces one can barely read, texts of physical beauty
(in words) that enact their own destruction and dispersion.
Mergings, as when words are almost double printed. . . . Or whole
shadow sounds . . . where the whole weight of Indo-European
consonant relations, not to speak of our culture's relations with the
underwritten, undersaid, socially repressed, becomes the fulcrum
for the line break. . . .

Here is DuPlessis's explanation:

She wants to show the half-seen, the half-forgotten. Her work is
filled with memories of abandonment; she represents the silence
half-sounded of the powerless. Her work is filled with the rhetorics
of philosophy and theology, and represents the sounds of power in
relation to doubt and silence. She is suspicious of languages and
discourses as already made and inhabited things; she wants to
enter and inhabit the untoward crevices of language. . . . (131–32)

Crevices, cracks, fissures—again and again these haunts are named,
moved into, inhabited in feminist critical writing, as if we are listening
there for the echoes of sound and thought. But is this kind of writing
feminist? Interestingly, poet and critic Susan Howe has deliberately
shunned certain kinds of feminism—specifically those singular claims
about women, those univocal claims about their writing. Turning away
from these tendencies, both Howe and DuPlessis write feminism as
more polyvocal—but not uncontrolled, chaotic, "babble."
    And this tenor of feminism is emphatically critical, in all its
rhythms and breaks and soundings. I have cited DuPlessis earlier, in the
Preface to my book, as taking her lead from Virginia Woolf who sought
"'a new critical method,' both 'colloquial and yet intense,' with the
swiftness and lightness of a 'sketch' but really 'a finished work'" (vii).
There is no mistaking the emphasis that DuPlessis places on this
"critical" dimension of polyvocality. Thinking of her own poetry, she
writes: "Must make a critical poetry, an analytic lyric . . . one which
questions the discourses. This situation makes of representation a site of
struggle" (145). And thinking of her criticism, she writes: "So it has
seemed crucial for feminist writing to reexamine and claim the
innovative heteroglossia, intergenres, and self-reflexivity (to name just

some) to our uses. Hence, in these works criticism and representation of thought is itself a site of struggle, and these works were, from their inception, examples of the cultural disturbance I evoked" (viii).

Poetic literacy. I think of it as not so much a balancing act, with equal parts of image and abstract idea, rhythmic sound and staid cadence, keeping us afoot. But rather, I think of it in terms that DuPlessis uses to describe an attempt "to articulate critical leverage in form or language . . ." (66). It is a kind of critical leverage one must maintain in the midst of ruptures, breaks, fissures within language. Not some simplistic outburst, but a more complex bursting open from within, often through tiny crevices—words, gaps in the sentence, unexpected sounds and rhythms—a reworking of the very medium of language for resignifications. Jane Tompkins wrote about her anger in terms of something hard, something "become adamantine, a black slab that glows in the dark." For DuPlessis and H.D., the volcano. Here is DuPlessis seeking critical leverage through this hardness, working that image into her language, argument:

> The practice of anguage. The anguish of language. The anger of language. (165)

Cracking open the word "language," taking away the initial "l," mixing into it the sheer sound of the word "anguish." This, for me, represents careful, cautious, critical leverage—not wildly running away from thought, but engaging the very practice of thought in its most suggestive and sounding dimensions. Citing Julia Kristeva, DuPlessis describes such leverage this way: "No pure semiotic . . . no pure semiotic. Exile. That is, mediation. Access to this area is mediated" (87).

I think back to Kristeva and these negotiations, mediations, between the symbolic and semiotic dispositions of language—one the controlling law of language, the other filled with sounds and rhythms, informing poetry. I think of her own theoretical writing, which at times taps into the "rhythmic, intonational repetitions" she associates with semiotic dispositions. This writing does not run away from the sonorous qualities of language that are typically consigned to some off-limits domains associated with madness, the unconscious, even the maternal and the feminine. Instead, as DuPlessis suggests, it "mediates" these forces in language, kneads them into a sounding literacy. At the end of her essay "Stabat Mater," Kristeva turns to the question of ethics, and wonders if we may be moving toward a different ethics—not one that turns its back on the law and moral code, but gives it "flesh, language and *jouissance*" (185). Her suggestion urges me to think of our moving, similarly, toward a different kind of critical literacy—not one that rushes away from the law of language, but gives it flesh, poetry, a way to deal with the very *process of thinking* that refuses to cast off these sounds to the repressed domain of the feminine and maternal, the mad and the unconscious.

In her poetic musings, Kristeva uses terms that I've found evocative of my own ideas about poetic language and literacy—about how it works and what it might engender: "But it is there, too, that the speaking being finds a refuge when his/her symbolic shell cracks and a crest emerges where speech causes biology to show through . . ." (185). I am reminded of spaces cracking open for sound to emerge, for DuPlessis, the parting of lips: "What is that big red mouth?" I would respond: it evokes a careful "mediation" of the dynamic forces in language: "Heterogeneous and self-questioning, judgmental and polyvalent, craving and craven—this is the practice" (66). This craving, this desire, recalls Kristeva's tentative but rather daring statement about poetic language and theory: "It is probably necessary to be a woman (ultimate guarantee of sociality beyond the wreckage of the paternal symbolic function, as well as the inexhaustible generator of its renewal, of its expansion) not to renounce theoretical reason but to compel it to increase its power by giving it an object beyond its limits. Such a position, it seems to me, provides a possible basis for a theory of signification, which, confronted with poetic language, could not in any way account for it, but would rather use it as an indication of what is heterogeneous to meaning . . ." (*Desire* 146).

It seems to me that all this is probably necessary—that the reformulation of theory has required the contribution of women, that in the case of feminist theory this contribution has required a distinctly poetic cast, that what we now have on our hands is the enactment, the actual practice, of this conjunction of theoretical reason and poetic language. Within feminist theory, the forces of this conjunction speak not some deep, indulgent desire in language, but a specific desire for language that can stretch significations, elicit and enact meanings.

Poetic literacy will not offer us some haven, give us all the right meanings and proper messages, feminist or otherwise. Far from that, it dispenses an antidote to prescriptive language by proffering a more abundant and sumptuous means through which we can negotiate meaning. We need language as abundant and convoluted and complex as culture; we need writing, especially modes of critical writing, through which we can work this thick language into theory—not to solidify firm feminist messages or to celebrate some vague polyvocal politics. We need it so that we can maneuver along the jagged edges of signification that feminism itself has uncovered: so we can move among many and multi-layered meanings, articulate and adjudicate bodily responses, negotiate narratives, engage a critical literacy that is questioning, craving, and crisp.

EPILOGUE: CRACKING THE O

IS THE MOTION OF SOUND
LIKE THOUGHT?

Cracking Eggs

Once, an orange cat
was so mixed up with the world
there was little room
for here, there, or wherefore-art-thou.

She assumed the claw-tooth rip in the sunset
from a branch in the apple tree,
and at dawn she pooled with light
on the pale pine floor.

She was that brief crack
when the world is perfect blend—
celebration of cat, bird, shrub—
before things jaggedly go their way.
                    —Katherine Soniat, *Cracking Eggs*

Throughout this book I have tried to listen for the sounds evoked by language, working the metaphor of the O from Olga Broumas's poem, hearing its resonances in critical writing. Early on I suggested that the motion of words is like sound, and that sounding language offers fuller sensory access to significations and meanings than prevailing metaphors of focused vision. In this epilogue, I want to work a slightly different aspect of this metaphor, and suggest that "cracking the O," much like "cracking eggs" in Soniat's poem, creates fissures in language that have been especially appealing to feminist theorists, sites where thought becomes unstable and therefore vulnerable to transformation.

Like the orange cat, we can become suddenly caught up in these cracks and crevices, so "mixed up with the world" that vision trans-forms reality into something seen differently: a tree branch becomes a rip in the sunset; light becomes a substance moving on the floor. Perception is altered through the play of light, much like Samuel Delany's "motion of light in water," much like Joan Scott's insistence that language works as a wavering medium reflecting and refracting what we perceive. I have suggested that the wavering motion of words resembles sound more than light, that its effects are more evocative and audible than visible and certain. When Susan Griffin speaks of "cracks in the surface" of language, when Rachael DuPlessis describes the parting of lips and the "crevices of language," when Julia Kristeva describes a time when the "symbolic shell cracks," I read them as listening for those moments when sound emerges in language and destabilizes thought. I read them as listening for sounds that change what we see and hear, and therefore what we can know. Just as our orange cat seizes a perfect opportunity for altered vision in a shadow cast by the sun, so I would suggest that feminist critics seize such opportunities in language along the cracks and fissures of meaning, as words and sounds move, as they "jaggedly go their way."

But the process can be as smooth as speech, as the mouth, as lips poised to speak—such a perfect moment. If, as Kristeva suspects, turns toward poetic language accompany "crises within social structures and institutions—the moments of their mutation, evolution, revolution, or disarray" (*Desire* 125), then I would add that feminist turns toward poetic language signal a particularly oral move within these crises. They speak into critical writing—through the parting of lips, through that big red mouth—the unsettling processes of sound and signification. Describing her own critical project, Kristeva insists that she does not collapse theory into art, and argues instead for "a theoretical discourse . . . resting on the brink of fiction without ever completely toppling over into it" (ix). I would argue that much of the feminist critical project also rests on such a brink, places where sound creates cracks and fissures in language, where we have opportunities to seize mutations in meanings.

These jagged edges—between theory and fiction, poetic and critical language, bodily pulsations and mindful ponderings—have emerged not only as a crucial site for feminist critical writing, but as the place where we share in a vital linguistic enterprise with others on the contemporary critical scene. By way of this epilogue, I would like to talk about this shared project, and particularly the role that feminist critics assume in negotiating the unsettled meanings that result from a volatile language. We are, after all, walking a fine line when we move away from the clarity and stability of language. On the other side is the threat of meaninglessness, babble, furious shouting or deafening silence. If the feminist writers I have brought together here offer any kind of common message, it would be the compelling necessity of negotiating our way along this brink.

While I sense a tendency among many contemporary theorists to be fascinated with, often intensely desirous of, the decenterings and destabilizations of writing, I find most of them ultimately afraid to engage its effects in critical prose. I say this not to cast aspersions on some distinctly male postmodern project, but to point to crucial differences in the ways that this complex project is articulated. In his pivotal essay "Structure, Sign, and Play in the Discourse of the Human Sciences," Jacques Derrida embraces the *"superabundance* of the signifier,"* endorsing a "Nietzschean *affirmation"* of "freeplay" in language. And yet he shies away from this very process, configuring it in terms of childbearing—"the *conception, the formation, the gestation, the labor,"* and putting himself in the company of those who "turn their eyes away in the face of the as yet unnameable which is proclaiming itself . . . only under the species of the non-species, in the formless, mute, infant, and terrifying form of monstrosity" (970–71).

These metaphors, of course, beg for a feminist reading. And yet I do not want to rush in and place feminist critics in the dubious position of discursive midwife. Something more complicated is at work here, and I believe it involves a kind of comfort, and indeed discomfort, felt about certain kinds of language and thought. When Derrida, for instance, turns to Nietzsche, along with Freud and Heidegger, as a pivotal voice in proclaiming the decentering of language and metaphysics, I am reminded of Nietzsche's own charged ambivalent responses to both women and language, and particularly this passage from *Thus Spoke Zarathustra* unfolding in a conversation with an old woman:

> Everything about woman is a riddle, and everything about woman has one solution: it is called pregnancy.
>
> For the woman, the man is a means: the end is always the child. But what is the woman for the man?
>
> The true man wants two things: danger and play. For that reason, he wants woman, as the most dangerous plaything.
>
> . . . .
>
> Then the little old woman answered me: "Zarathustra has said many nice things, especially for those who are young enough for them. [. . .]

"And now accept as thanks a little truth! I am certainly old enough for it!

"Wrap it up and stop its mouth: otherwise it will cry too loudly, this little truth!"

"Give me your little truth, woman!" I said. And thus spoke the little old woman:

"Are you visiting a woman? Do not forget your whip!" (275–76)

I cite this passage not only to show what I take to be Nietzsche's contorted desire and fear of the womanly "mouth," his apparent simultaneous longing and loathing for this dangerous cry, but also as an opportunity to show how a feminist writer might respond to this desirous fear: of the riddle, the pregnancy, the endlessly uttering mouth. Luce Irigaray writes back to him in her book *Marine Lover of Friedrich Nietzsche*:

And you had all to lose sight of me so I could come back, toward you, with an other gaze.

And, certainly, the most arduous thing has been to seal my lips, out of love. To close off this mouth that has always sought to flow free.

But, had I never held back, never would you have remembered that something exists which has a language other than your own. That, from her prison, someone was calling out to return to the air. That your words reasoned all the better because within them a voice was captive. Amplifying your speech with an endless resonance.

I was your resonance. (3)

Just how much flow, how much resonance, can be accommodated in critical thought? Between shutting up the mouth, and letting loose a flood of utterances—where exactly on the brink can feminist theory, or any theory, sustain its tenuous positionings? To a large extent, these questions echo all around the destabilization of language in contemporary critical theory. And, to a large extent, they figure themselves through reference to the mouth, to speech, to the oral dynamics of dialogue and polyvocality—the sheer motion of language and thought.

Consider this remarkable passage from Heidegger, another figure cited by Derrida as proclaiming decentered language and metaphysics:

> It is just as much a property of language to sound and ring and vibrate, to hover and to tremble, as it is for the spoken words of language to carry a meaning. But our experience of this property is still exceedingly clumsy, because the metaphysical-technological explanation gets everywhere in the way, and keeps us from considering the matter properly. . . .
>
> But the mouth is not merely a kind of organ of the body under-stood as an organism—body and mouth are part of the earth's flow and growth in which we mortals flourish, and from which we receive the soundness of our roots. . . .
>
> Language is the flower of the mouth. (98-99)

And this, from the final pages of Barthes's *The Pleasure of the Text*:

> If it were possible to imagine an aesthetic of textual pleasure, it would have to include: *writing aloud.* . . . what it searches for (in a perspective of bliss) are the pulsional incidents, the language lined with flesh, a text where we can hear the grain of the throat, the patina of consonants, the voluptuousness of vowels, a whole carnal stereophony: the articulation of the body, of the tongue. . . . (66–67)

This reconfiguration of thought and writing in terms of speech, in the contexts and resonances of sound, may well constitute one of the most important turns in contemporary intellectual traditions. Describing this phenomenon in a broad range of what he calls "difference-sensitive theory," Wlad Godzich in his recent book *The Culture of Literacy* says that this theory has "recognized and thematized something that had escaped earlier thought: the cry . . . a philosophy of the cry. . ." (26).

Yes, there is the cry. But then there is also that big red mouth. When I recall how Godzich deliberately ignores feminist theory in his otherwise provocative book, it becomes easier for me to distinguish between the philosophical cry and the big red mouth, the abstract sound and the careful parting of lips. Who is really "writing aloud" in theory, taking in language as "the flower of the mouth"?

When DuPlessis asks, "What is that big red mouth?" I want to answer that it is the site where a "cry" materializes in theory, where a cry becomes a critical utterance. It is a crucial parting of lips in language—a kind of cracking motion, a fissure—through which sounding utterances shatter and erode established meanings. If much contemporary theory concerns itself with ideas about cries and vocalizations and linguistic destabilization, I would proffer that feminist theory distinguishes itself by mouthing these vocalizations in critical writing. When, addressing her words to Nietzsche, Irigaray says "I am your resonance," I read her as articulating messages that resound inside language and thought, listening and reflection. Instead of calling for some new writing, I hear her urging on the resonance *within* theoretical discourse that would imbue it with an altogether different tenor, with vocal amplifications and reverberating significations that make theory into something more like Rich's poetic language, thick with messages. Not some chaotic outburst, but a working and kneading of sound into written language and critical thought for the very purposes of expanding and multiplying possible meanings. The articulation and negotiation of these possibilities, I believe, marks a distinctive feminist enactment within the language of contemporary theory.

In saying this, I would shift metaphors for feminist voice away from that of monster or Medusa or even "big red mouth" (as appealing as these remain for me), and suggest that we might well configure the feminist critical engagement in language in terms of a rather dexterous speaker, or perhaps a dexterous mover, like our orange cat seizing opportunities. The voice of this speaker would indeed be one that resonates, but also one, as Cixous says, that is hardly "without a minimum of philosophical and analytical knowledge" ("Exchange" 147). For all the sound and fury surrounding claims to feminist voice, Irigaray reminds us that fear of such voices has been far more furious than the voices themselves. Someone always seems to be rushing in to "stop its mouth" for fear that it will "cry too loudly." Paranoia about the potential excesses of language is everywhere. Indeed Foucault took this fear as the continuing subject of his critical agenda. In his "Discourse on Language" he explains the varied "forms and modes" in which language is controlled, as if society is continually responding to "a profound logophobia, a sort of dumb fear of these events, of this mass of spoken things, of everything that could possibly be violent, discontinuous, querulous, disordered even and perilous in it, of the incessant, disorderly buzzing of discourse" (228–29).

But let us get more specific. In what ways, we might wonder, does contemporary critical theory celebrate the "cry" of discourse while still itself fearing to engage its resonance? If we merely describe these sounds, without actually enacting them, then we may lose the opportunity to insinuate such sounding language within critical writing, and lose as well the chance to negotiate our way beyond the inevitably bifurcated scenarios of reasoned prose or hysterical voice. In the contexts and themes of contemporary critical theory, that loss would be inestimable.

Too much is at stake, not only for certain groups of people who make certain claims about language, but for the future of critical and theoretical language, for the "crisis" that Kristeva describes whose very "agent" of "fermentation" is language itself (*Language* 329). Theory stands to be significantly altered when its articulations sound more poetic, when its messages are more audibly provocative. It might invest intellectual energies at once in abstraction, analysis, and ambiguity; its meanings might lead to steady determinations even as they proffer multiple, paradoxical alternatives. Critical discourse might, as Woolf desired, move toward precision and flight.

There are numerous fissures and cracks—perfect opportunities, like those presented to our cat at sunset and dawn—to pry open and loosen the firm ground that keeps thetic and poetic, thoughtfully quiet and resoundingly pulsating qualities of language cast in their respective places. With this loosening, linguistic territories begin to mutate and erode. Words move, becoming far less stable in their signification than we once thought. The motion of words alters meanings that have been taken for granted, that begin to sound differently. The motion of sound is like thought itself—a wavering, changeable substance.

We need negotiation through this scary yet promising territory. Pondering the possibilities of writing within what she describes as "transnational, intercultural, feminist literacy," Donna Haraway calls for "articulation," the mutative powers of speech in a world that has "always been in the middle of things, in unruly and practical conversation . . ." ("Monsters" 327, 304). Working the metaphor of biological articulata, creatures "full of sensory hairs, evaginations, invaginations, and indentations," she writes: "To articulate is to signify. It is to put things together, scary things, risky things, contingent things" (324).

I think of creatures with mouths and lips, amazingly articulate, working their way through necessary negotiations within unruly yet always thoughtful critical conversations. This is not the abyss. This is the brink, the edge, where the O cracks and a resounding language alters what we hear, and see, and know. What I have written here carves out a space around this cracking surface. It is not some new linguistic territory that promises salvation through sound, or provides easy liberation from the long exclusive traditions of cultural literacy. But this space, hollowed out like an echo, shows where feminist writers have brought language to its limits and lips, and put it to work—in the uneasy yet imperative realm of negotiations that constitute critical thought.

NOTES

Preface

1. I refer to Irigaray's general critique of a specular philosophy in *Speculum of the Other Woman*, as well as her specific essay "The Looking Glass, from the Other Side" in *This Sex Which Is Not One*. The initial section of Trinh's *Woman, Native, Other* is entitled "Commitment from the Mirror-Writing Box." Although Silverman's attention to "female voice" in cinema develops in contexts different from my own, she rightly remarks that theorists have failed to notice how "sexual difference is the effect of dominant cinema's sound regime as well as its visual regime" (viii). Haraway's ideas on "partial vision" are best expressed in her essay "Situated Knowledges" in *Simians, Cyborgs, and Women*. I cite the reference to de Lauretis, actually, from Paula Bennett's essay "Critical Clitoridectomy," where debates about the varied hidden, veiled, and visible symbolic presence of the clitoris inform arguments about both feminist criticism and women's writing.

2. I think especially of Julia Kristeva's notion of a "semiotic disposition" in language, which rebounds with the sounding, rhythmic pulsations of the chora. See the essays in *Desire in Language*, to which I will return in subsequent chapters.

3. My references here are to Sedgwick's response to her essay on "Jane Austen and the Masturbating Girl" (*Against Epistemology* 134); Irigaray's *Marine Lover of Friedrich Nietzsche* 3); Williams's *Alchemy of Race and Rights*; Kristeva's essays throughout *Desire in Language*, but particularly "From One Identity to Another"; and Haraway's essay "The Promises of Monsters."

4. This metaphor extends at least from Plato to Derrida, and extends throughout varied deconstructive readings of texts. Perhaps its most fascinating articulation is in Lacan's and Derrida's analysis of Edgar Allen Poe's "The Purloined Letter," where language itself is endlessly stolen and we are all detectives in pursuit of meaning. See Barbara Johnson's analysis of this predicament in her essay "The Frame of Reference."

5. My reference is to the work of Marshall McLuhan, though he was not necessarily so optimistic in describing the effects of a technologically connected "global village."

1. Vocal Critics

1. The effects of such sounding poetic devices as meter, alliteration, and rhyme and rhythm permeate diverse literary traditions. The distinctly "dialogic" and "polyvocal" qualities of the novel have formed the subject of Bakhtin's theories. More recently, an appreciation for the oral dimensions of distinctive ethnic literatures, such as African American and Native American, have opened new ways for reading and studying their texts, as critical works such as Henry Louis Gates's *The Signifying Monkey* and Greg Sarris's *Keeping Slug Woman Alive* readily show.

2. I have turned to Ong for his concise descriptions of oral language and thought even as I want to keep in mind that such pronounced distinctions between orality and literacy have been called into question. Those who have reiterated the so-called "great divide" theories see oral cultures as fundamentally different from literate ones in the kinds of language and consciousness they sustain. Others are less inclined to see the difference as so pronounced, and emphasize instead the complex interplay between language associated with purely oral and purely literate communication. Nonetheless, clarifying these distinctions has encouraged insights into oral-literate mergings and mixtures, not the least of which is the peculiar kind of sounding critique produced by the feminist theorists I will be discussing in this book. As Ruth Finnegan explains in rejecting what she calls the "great divide" theories about orality and literacy, such theories are nonetheless "worth reflecting" especially if they are "used critically as starting points rather than as comprehensive answers" that might "lead us to important issues for investigation. . . ." In this sense, understanding oral-literate contrasts may deepen our understanding of what Finnegan calls "the interaction of oral and written forms as a regular and unsurprising process across a multidimensional continuum, rather than as something which involves bridging some deep divide" (xii–xiii). De Certeau strikes a similar note when he describes a "Scriptural Economy": "I want to make it clear at the outset that in referring to writing and orality I am not postulating two opposed terms whose contradiction could be transcended by a third, or whose hierarchization could be inverted. . . . They are incommensurable; the difference between them is qualitative" (133). Whatever one's position, the delineation and awareness of oral-literate contrasts have contributed in specific ways to our understanding of the crucial role, as anthropologist Jack Goody explains, that "the means and relations of communication" play in shaping thought, culture, and social organization (175)—a now widely accepted poststructuralist tenet.

3. Ong's suspicions bear striking similarity to the observations of Elene Kolb, who relates how women troubadours spoke through their songs after having been denied access to the learned languages of Greek and Latin. In the process, these women preserved the spoken, vernacular language that had little

to do with the artificial style of classical poets and the rhetorical training of the bureaucrat. What did they write? "Nothing like that written in the established classical languages, which had words for abstractions and philosophical terms and nuances that the new, young vernaculars didn't yet have. This women's writing was concrete, colloquial, filled with ordinary detail and sensuous—characteristics that had as much to do with the languages in which it was written as the fact that women were writing it" (29). Also see Meg Bogin's work, cited by Margaret Randall as part of the "new female voice" as it speaks "in overlay" with women's voices from the past (*Walking* 45). Laurie Finke shows how such language differences reflected not some essential qualities of women's language, but women's "different investments in the social relations of *fin' amor*, their different social positions, which are ideologically determined by the social construction of gender" (49). King's chapter on the oral and the written in her book *Theory in Its Feminist Travels* takes her in directions different from my own, especially as she focuses on "writing technologies"—from languages to the material means of publication—that derive from what she calls "the elusive and politically charged boundaries between the oral and the written" (104). Also see her essay "Feminism and Writing Technologies."

4. In his study of "soundscapes," Murray Schafer explains how the advent of writing and especially print in the west elevated vision over sound, resulting in our increasing lack of sensitivity not only to the sounds that surround us, but our very abilities to know the world through listening to its sounds as voices (11). This primacy given to vision is hardly characteristic of many if not most nonwestern cultures. For a fascinating study of how meanings and relationships are communicated through sound in the rainforest environment of the Kaluli people of Papua New Guinea, see Steven Feld's work.

5. While Foley's studies are devoted to oral works, I would advocate much the same approach for literate texts. In this spectrum, we could turn to a range of written works, from those in which the dynamics of oral language seem entirely absent to those in which the distinctive effects of oral and written language become intertwined. Deborah Tannen explains that the advent of literacy does not simply erase orality, but instead "the two are superimposed upon and intertwined with each other" in ways that reflect the dynamics of particular settings and contexts, producing what she calls an "oral/literate continuum" (3). We might trace this continuum throughout a variety of communication, as Robin Tolmach Lakoff does when she finds the "mingling of oral and literate strategies" in certain literary texts, and describes a general "shift" in our media-oriented society "from a literacy-based model of ideal human communication to one based on the oral mode of discourse" ("The Mingling" 240). Indeed the study of oral dimensions of technological media—especially television, video, film, and more recently the computer—has generated numerous speculations about oral infusions into our high-tech literate culture.

3. Resounding Bodies

1. Jacqueline Zita's review article in *Signs* attempts to come to terms with the plentiful and yet continually perplexing ideas about the body in just four recent books that address the subject. Long ignored, repressed, and devalued in intellectual traditions, the body now seems to be everywhere, as the editors of the volume *Thinking Bodies* explain: "Change is in the wind. . . . there is clearly a renewal of philosophical interest in how bodies think, how thought is embodied" (6). While my arguments hone in more specifically on body writing, they obviously partake in this rich reassessment of what the body means, and can mean, in intellectual traditions.

2. Numerous scholarly works devoted to oral-literate contrasts discuss the connections between oral language and body movements. See Ong's commentary and references on this matter (*Orality and Literacy* 34, 67–68). For a particularly fascinating study of women's narrative performances and their connection to hand and body gesturing, see Harold Scheub's essay on "Body and Image" among the Xhosa women of South Africa.

3. Patricia Hill Collins makes a similar point when she argues that Black women's blues traditions constitute an important dimension of *Black Feminist Thought*. Emphasizing the oral dimensions of this tradition, she describes the blues as assuming "a similar function in African-American oral culture as that played by print media for white, visually based culture" (99).

4. For example, see Judith Butler's comments in *Bodies That Matter* (41, 69–71), and Kaja Silverman's different claim that despite her writings on the maternal and semiotic, Kristeva ultimately writes through "the male voice" (113).

5. See especially Kristeva's essays on art and literature in *Desire in Language*. Although my references, via Kristeva and Suleiman, are mainly literary, scholars in other disciplines have produced compelling accounts of maternal language. See, for example, the work of Marta Weigle, who explores the actual language of myths and birthing across diverse cultures, and draws on Dennis Tedlock's distinction between *"logos"* and *"dialogos"* to describe the language of midwifery. While logos emanates from a solitary distanced voice, the language of procreation here generates from multiple voices of women in dialogue, midwives whose talk is infused with rhythms and chants. I cannot help but note the resemblance between these voices and those in certain gnostic texts, as analyzed by Pagels, voices that emanate from within everyone.

WORKS CITED

Allen, Jeffner. "Poetic Politics: How the Amazons Took the Acropolis." *Sexual Practice. Textual Theory: Lesbian Cultural Criticism.* Ed. Susan J. Wolfe and Julia Penelope. Cambridge, Mass.: Blackwell, 1993. 307-21.

———. *reverberations across the shimmering CASCADAS*. Albany: State U of New York P, 1994.

Allen, Paula Gunn. *The Sacred Hoop: Recovering the Feminine in American Indian Traditions.* Boston: Beacon Press, 1986.

Anzaldúa, Gloria. *Borderlands LaFrontera: The New Mestiza.* San Francisco: Spinsters/Aunt Lute, 1987.

———, ed. *Making Face, Making Soul: Haciendo Caras.* San Francisco: Aunt Lute, 1990.

Baker, Houston. "Caliban's Triple Play." *"Race," Writing, and Difference.* Ed. Henry Louis Gates, Jr. Chicago: U of Chicago P, 1986. 381–95.

Bakhtin, M. M. *The Dialogic Imagination.* Ed. Michael Holquist, Trans. Caryl Emerson and Michael Holquist. Austin: U of Texas P, 1981.

Barthes, Roland. *The Pleasure of the Text.* Trans. Richard Miller. New York: Noonday Press, 1975.

———. *S/Z.* Trans. Richard Miller. New York: Hill and Wang, 1974.

———. *Writing Degree Zero.* Trans. Annette Lavers and Colin Smith. New York: Hill and Wang, 1968.

Bennett, Paula. "Critical Clitoridectomy: Female Sexual Imagery and Feminist Psychoanalytic Theory." *Signs: Journal of Women in Culture and Society* 18 (1993): 235–59.

Bhabha, Homi. "Postcolonial Authority and Postmodern Guilt." *Cultural Studies.* Ed. Lawrence Grossberg, Cary Nelson, and Paula Treichler. New York: Routledge, 1992. 56–68.

Bogin, Meg. *The Women Troubadors.* New York: Paddington Press, 1976.

Boyarin, Jonathan, ed. *The Ethnography of Reading.* Berkeley: U of California P, 1993.

Brooke-Rose, Christine. *Stories, Theories and Things*. Cambridge: Cambridge UP, 1991.

Broumas, Olga. *Beginning With O*. New Haven: Yale UP, 1977.

Burke, Carolyn. "Rethinking the Maternal." *The Future of Difference*. Ed. Hester Eisenstein and Alice Jardine. New Brunswick, N.J.: Rutgers UP, 1985. 107–14.

Butler, Judith. (1994). "A Skeptical Feminist Postscript to the Postmodern." *Postmodernism Across the Ages*. Ed. Bill Readings and Bennet Schaber. Syracuse, N.Y.: Syracuse UP, 233–37.

———. "Imitation and Gender Insubordination." *Inside/Out: Lesbian Theories, Gay Theories*. Ed. Diana Fuss. New York: Routledge, 1991. 13-31.

———. *Bodies That Matter: On the Discursive Limits of "Sex."* New York: Routledge, 1993.

———. *Gender Trouble: Feminism and the Subversion of Identity*. New York: Routledge, 1990.

Byatt, A. S. "The Next Room." *Sugar and Other Stories*. New York: Vintage, 1987.

Cameron, Deborah, ed. *The Feminist Critique of Language*. London: Routledge, 1990.

Christian, Barbara. *Black Feminist Criticism*. New York: Pergamon, 1985.

Cixous, Hélène. "An Exchange with Hélène Cixous." *Hélène Cixous: Writing the Feminine*. Verena Conley. Lincoln: U of Nebraska P, 1984.

———. "Forward." Trans. Verena Conley. *The Stream of Life*. By Clarice Lispector. Minneapolis: U of Minnesota P, 1989.

———. "The Laugh of the Medusa." *New French Feminisms*. Ed. Elaine Marks and Isabelle de Courtivron. New York: Schocken Books, 1981. 245–64.

Dempster, Elizabeth. "Women Writing the Body: Let's Watch a Little How She Dances." *Grafts: Feminist Cultural Criticism*. Ed. Susan Sheridan. London: Verso, 1988. 35–54.

de Certeau, Michel. *The Practice of Everyday Life*. Trans. Steven Rendall. Berkeley: U of California P, 1984.

Derrida, Jacques. "Structure, Sign, and Play in the Discourse of the Human Sciences." Trans. Richard Macksey and Eugenio Donato. *The Critical Tradition*. Ed. David H. Richter. New York: St. Martin's Press, 1989. 959–71.

de Lauretis, Teresa. "Feminist Studies/Critical Studies: Issues, Terms, and Contexts." *Feminist Studies/Critical Studies*. Ed. de Lauretis. Bloomington: Indiana UP, 1986. 1–19.

————. *The Practice of Love: Lesbian Sexuality and Perverse Desire*. Bloomington: Indiana UP, 1994.

DuPlessis, Rachael Blau. *The Pink Guitar: Writing as Feminist Practice*. New York: Routledge, 1990.

————. *Writing Beyond the Ending*. Bloomington: Indiana UP, 1985.

Eagleton, Terry. *Literary Theory: An Introduction*. Minneapolis: U of Minnesota P, 1983.

Eisenstein, Elizabeth. *The Printing Press as an Agent of Change*. 2 vols. New York: Cambridge UP, 1979.

Feld, Steven. *Sound and Sentiment: Birds, Weeping, Poetics, and Song in Kaluli Expression*. Philadelphia: U of Pennsylvania P, 1990.

Fetterley, Judith. *The Resisting Reader*. Bloomington: Indiana UP, 1977.

Finke, Laurie. *Feminist Theory, Women's Writing*. Ithaca, N.Y.: Cornell UP, 1992.

Finnegan, Ruth. *Literacy and Orality: Studies in the Technology of Communication*. Oxford: Basil Blackwell, 1988.

————. *Oral Poetry: Its Nature, Significance and Social Context*. 1977. Bloomington: Indiana UP, 1992.

Flax, Jane. *Disputed Subjects: Essays on Psychoanalysis, Politics and Philosophy*. New York: Routledge, 1993.

Foley, John Miles. *The Singer of Tales in Performance*. Bloomington: Indiana UP, 1995.

Foucault, Michel. *The Archaeology of Knowledge and the Discourse on Language*. Trans. A. M. Sheridan Smith. New York: Pantheon Books, 1972.

Freedman, Diane P. *An Alchemy of Genres: Cross-Genre Writing by American Feminist Poet-Critics*. Charlottesville: UP of Virginia, 1992.

Fuss, Diana, ed. *Inside/Out: Lesbian Theories, Gay Theories*. New York: Routledge, 1991.

Gallop, Jane. *Thinking Through the Body*. New York: Columbia UP, 1988.

Gates, Henry Louis. *The Signifying Monkey*. New York: Oxford UP, 1988.

Genette, Gérard. *Narrative Discourse*. Trans. Jane E. Lewin. Ithaca: Cornell UP, 1980.

Gilligan, Carol. *In a Different Voice*. Cambridge, Mass.: Harvard UP, 1982.

Godzich, Wlad. *The Culture of Literacy*. Cambridge, Mass.: Harvard UP, 1994.

Goody, Jack. *The Interface Between the Written and the Oral.* Cambridge: Cambridge UP, 1987.

———. *The Logic of Writing and the Organization of Society.* Cambridge: Cambridge UP, 1986.

Griffin, Susan. "Red Shoes." *The Politics of the Essay: Feminist Perspectives.* Ed. Ruth-Ellen Boetcher Joers and Elizabeth Mittman. Bloomington: Indiana UP, 1993. 1–11.

———. *Woman and Nature.* New York: Harper and Row, 1978.

Grosz, Elizabeth. "Refiguring Lesbian Desire." *The Lesbian Postmodern.* Ed. Laura Doan. New York: Columbia UP, 1994. 67-84.

———. *Volatile Bodies: Toward a Corporeal Feminism.* Bloomington: Indiana UP, 1994.

Hall, Stuart. "Cultural Studies and Its Theoretical Legacies." *Cultural Studies.* Ed. Lawrence Gorssberg, Cary Nelson, and Paula Treichler. New York: Routledge, 1992. 277-94.

Haraway, Donna. *Primate Visions: Gender, Race, and Nature in the World of Modern Science.* New York: Routledge, 1989.

———. "Primatology is Politics by Other Means." *Feminist Approaches to Science.* Ed. Ruth Bleier. New York: Pergamon Press, 1988. 77–118.

———. "The Promises of Monsters: A Regenerative Politics for Inappropriate/d Others." *Cultural Studies.* Ed. Lawrence Grossberg, Cary Nelson, and Paula Treichler. New York: Routledge, 1992. 295-337.

———. *Simians, Cyborgs, and Women: The Reinvention of Nature.* New York: Routledge, 1991.

Havelock, Eric. *The Muse Learns to Write: Reflections on Orality and Literacy from Antiquity to the Present.* New Haven: Yale UP, 1986.

———. "The Oral-Literate Equation: A Formula for the Modern Mind." *Literacy and Orality.* Ed. David R. Olson and Nancy Torrance. Cambridge: Cambridge UP, 1991.

Hedley, Jane. "Surviving to Speak New Language: Mary Daly and Adrienne Rich." *Hypatia* 7 (Spring 1992): 40–62.

Heidegger, Martin. *On the Way to Language.* Trans. Peter D. Hertz. San Francisco: Harper SanFrancisco, 1971.

Hirsch, E. D. *Cultural Literacy.* New York: Vintage, 1988.

hooks, bell. *Talking Back: Thinking Feminist, Thinking Black.* Boston: South End Press, 1989.

Irigaray, Luce. *Marine Lover of Friedrich Nietzsche.* Trans. Gillian C. Gill. New York: Columbia UP, 1991.

———. *This Sex Which Is Not One.* Trans. Catherine Porter. Ithaca, N.Y.: Cornell UP, 1985.

———. "Women's Exile. Interview with Luce Irigaray." Trans. Couze Venn. *The Feminist Critique of Language.* Ed. Deborah Cameron. London: Routledge, 1990. 80–96.

Joeres, Ruth-Ellen Boetcher and Elizabeth Mittman, eds. *The Politics of the Essay: Feminist Perspectives.* Bloomington: Indiana UP, 1993.

Johnson, Barbara. "The Frame of Reference: Poe, Lacan, Derrida." *Literature and Psychoanalysis.* Ed. Shoshana Felman. Baltimore: Johns Hopkins UP, 1982. 457–505.

Kaplan, Carla. *The Erotics of Talk: Women's Writing and Feminist Paradigms.* New York: Oxford UP, 1996.

King, Katie. "Feminism and Writing Technologies: Teaching Queerish Travels through Maps, Territories, and Pattern." *Configurations,* 2 (1): 89–106.

———. *Theory in Its Feminist Travels.* Bloomington: Indiana UP, 1994.

Kingston, Maxine Hong. "The Novel's Next Step." *Mother Jones* Dec. 1989: 37–41.

Koestenbaum, Wayne. "The Queen's Throat: (Homo)sexuality and the Art of Singing." *Inside/Out.* Ed. Diana Fuss. New York: Routledge, 1991. 205–34.

Kolb, Elene. "When Women Finally Got the Word." *New York Times Book Review,* 9 July 1989: 1, 28–29.

Kristeva, Julia. *Desire in Language: A Semiotic Approach to Literature and Art,* ed. Leon S. Roudiez, trans. Thomas Gora, Alice Jardine, and Leon S. Roudiez. New York: Columbia UP, 1980.

———. *Language: The Unknown.* Trans. Anne M. Menke. New York: Columbia UP, 1989.

———. *The Kristeva Reader.* Ed. Toril Moi. New York: Columbia UP, 1986.

Lakoff, Robin Tolmach. "Some of my Favorite Writers are Literate: The Mingling of Oral and Literate Strategies in Written Communication." *Spoken and Written Language.* Ed. Deborah Tannen. Norwood, N.J.: ABLEX, 1982. 239–60.

———. *Language and Woman's Place.* New York: Harper & Row, 1975.

Lorde, Audre. *Sister Outsider.* New York: The Crossing Press, 1984.

Lyotard, Jean-François. *The Postmodern Condition: A Report on Knowledge*. Trans. Geoff Bennington and Brian Massumi. Theory and History of Literature 10. Minneapolis: U of Minnesota P, 1984.

MacCannell, Juliet and Laura Zakarin, eds. *Thinking Bodies*. Stanford: Stanford UP, 1994.

Marks, Elaine. "Lesbian Intertextuality." *Sexual Practice/Textual Theory: Lesbian Cultural Criticism*. Ed. Susan J. Wolfe and Julia Penelope. Cambridge, Mass.: Blackwell, 1993. 271–90.

Martin, Wallace. *Recent Theories of Narrative*. Ithaca, N.Y.: Cornell UP, 1986.

McLuhan, Marshall. *The Gutenberg Galaxy: The Making of Typographic Man*. Toronto: Toronto UP, 1962.

———, with Quentin Fiore. *The Medium Is the Massage*. New York: Bantam, 1967.

Meese, Elizabeth. *(Sem)Erotics: Theorizing Lesbian : Writing*. New York: New York UP, 1992.

Miller, Nancy K. *Getting Personal: Feminist Occasions and Other Autobiographical Acts*. New York: Routledge, 1991.

Nietzsche, Friedrich. From *Thus Spoke Zarathustra*. *A Nietzsche Reader*. Selected and trans. R. J. Hollingdale. New York: Penguin, 1977.

Nye, Andrea. *Words of Power*. New York: Routledge, 1990.

Ong, Walter. *Orality and Literacy: The Technologizing of the Word*. London: Methuen, 1982.

Pagels, Elaine. *The Gnostic Gospels*. New York: Vintage, 1981.

———. "What Became of God the Mother? Conflicting Images of God in Early Christianity." *The Signs Reader: Women, Gender & Scholarship*. Ed. Elizabeth Abel and Emily K. Abel. Chicago: U of Chicago P, 1983. 97–107.

Parker, Alice. "Under the Covers: A Synesthesia of Desire (Lesbian Translations)." *Sexual Practice/Textual Theory: Lesbian Cultural Criticism*. Ed. Susan J. Wolfe and Julia Penelope. Cambridge, Mass.: Blackwell, 1993. 322–39.

Peabody, Berkley. *The Winged Word: A Study in the Technique of Ancient Greek Oral Composition as Seen Principally through Hesiod's Works and Days*. Albany: State U of New York P, 1975.

Plato, *The Republic*. Excerpts from *Literary Criticism and Theory: The Greeks to the Present*. Ed. Robert Con Davis and Laurie Finke. New York: Longman, 1989.

Randall, Margaret. *Dancing with the Doe: New and Selected Poems 1986–1991.* Albuquerque, N.M.: West End Press, 1992.

Rich, Adrienne. "Compulsory Heterosexuality and Lesbian Existence." *The Signs Reader.* Ed. Elizabeth Abel and Emily K. Abel. Chicago: U of Chicago P, 1983. 139–68.

———. *Diving into the Wreck: Poems 1971–1972.* New York: Norton, 1973.

———. "'It is the Lesbian in Us . . .'" *On Lies, Secrets, and Silence: Selected Prose 1966–1978.* New York: Norton, 1979. 199–202.

———. "Notes Toward a Politics of Location." *Blood, Bread, and Poetry: Selected Prose, 1979–1985.* New York: Norton, 1986.

———. *What Is Found There: Notebooks on Poetry and Politics.* New York: Norton, 1993.

Roman, Camille, Suzanne Juhasz, and Cristanne Miller, eds., *The Women and Language Debate.* New Brunswick, N.J.: Rutgers UP, 1994.

Roof, Judith. *A Lure of Knowledge: Lesbian Sexuality and Theory.* New York: Columbia UP, 1991.

———. "The Match in the Crocus: Representations of Lesbian Sexuality." *Discontented Discourses: Feminism/Textual Intervention/Psychoanalysis.* Ed. Marleen S. Barr and Richard Feldstein. Urbana: U of Illinois P, 1989. 100–116.

Salvaggio, Ruth. "Theory and Space, Space and Woman." *Tulsa Studies in Women's Literature.* 7, 2 (1988): 261–82.

Sarris, Greg. *Keeping Slug Woman Alive.* Berkeley: U of California P, 1993.

Schafer, R. Murray. (1980). *The Tuning of the World: Toward a Theory of Soundscape Design.* Philadelphia: U of Pennsylvania P, 1980.

Scheub, Harold. (1977). "Body and Image in Oral Narrative Performance." *New Literary History* 8 (1977): 345–67.

Scott, Joan. "The Evidence of Experience." in *Questions of Evidence.* Ed. James Chandler, Arnold I. Davidson, Harry Harootunian. Chicago: U of Chicago P, 1991. 363-87.

———. *Gender and the Politics of History.* New York: Columbia UP, 1988.

Sedgwick, Eve Kosofsky. "Against Epistemology." In *Questions of Evidence.* Ed. James Chandler, Arnold I. Davidson, Harry Harootunian. Chicago: U of Chicago P, l991. 132–36.

———. *Tendencies.* Durham, N.C.: Duke UP, 1993.

Silko, Leslie Marmon. *Ceremony.* New York: Penguin, 1977.

Silverman, Kaja. *The Acoustic Mirror: The Female Voice in Psychoanalysis and Cinema.* Bloomington: Indiana UP, 1988.

Soniat, Katherine. *Cracking Eggs.* Orlando: U of Central Florida P, 1990.

Sprengnether, Madelon. "Ghost Writing: A Meditation on Literary Criticism as Narrative." *Transitional Objects and Potential Spaces: Literary Uses of D. W. Winnicott.* Ed. Peter L. Rudnytsky. New York: Columbia UP, 1993.

Suleiman, Susan Rubin. "Writing and Motherhood." *The Mother Tongue: Essays in Feminist Psychoanalytic Interpretation.* Ed. Shirley Nelson Garner, Claire Kahane, and Madelon Sprengnether. Ithaca, N.Y.: Cornell UP, 1985. 352–77.

Tannen, Deborah. "The Oral/Literate Continuum in Dicourse." *Spoken and Written Language: Exploring Orality and Literacy.* Norwood, New Jersey: ABLEX, 1982. 1–16.

Tompkins, Jane. "Me and My Shadow." *Gender and Theory: Dialogues on Feminist Criticism.* Ed. Linda Kauffman. Oxford: Basil Blackwell, 1989. 121–39.

Trinh T. Minh-ha. *When the Moon Waxes Red: Representation, Gender and Cultural Politics.* New York: Routledge, 1991.

———. *Woman, Native, Other: Writing Postcoloniality and Feminism.* Bloomington: Indiana UP, 1989.

Weigle, Marta. *Creation and Procreation: Feminist Reflections on Mythologies of Cosmogony and Parturition.* Philadelphia: U of Pennsylvania P, 1989.

White, Hayden. *The Content of the Form.* Baltimore: Johns Hopkins UP, 1987.

Williams, Patricia. *The Alchemy of Race and Rights: Diary of a Law Professor.* Cambridge, Mass.: Harvard UP, 1991.

Wittig, Monique. *The Lesbian Body.* Trans. David LeVay. New York: William Morrow, 1975.

———. *The Straight Mind and Other Essays.* Boston: Beacon Press, 1992.

Woodward, Carolyn. "'My Heart So Wrapt': Lesbian Disruptions in Eighteenth-Century Fiction." *Signs: Journal of Women in Culture and Society* 18 (1993): 838–65.

Woolf, Virginia. *A Room of One's Own.* 1929. San Diego: Harcourt, Brace, Jovanovich, 1957.

———. *A Writer's Diary.* New York: Harcourt, Brace, 1954.

———. *Mrs. Dalloway.* New York: Harcourt, Brace and World, 1925.

Zita, Jacqueline. Review of *Making Bodies, Making History*, by Leslie Adelson, *Unbearable Weight*, by Susan Bordo, *Bodies That Matter*, by Judith Butler, and *Volatile Bodies*, by Elizabeth Grosz. *Signs: Journal of Women in Culture and Society* 21 (1996): 786–95.

INDEX

moved at lightning speed in two quick movements. Stags' eyes looked down to see blood on his hand and the Juicer cleaning his Vibro-Blades on his leather vest. Insults leapt to Stags' tongue, but never materialized as his rat-like head separated from his neck and his body fell limp.

"What kind of bonus was that?" asked Goliath.

Viper smirked and shrugged his shoulders.

"He didn't suffer, I guess," replied the Juicer as he began to chuckle. Goliath chuckled too.

"So what's the plan?" he asked.

Viper's smirk turned into a toothy grin.

"Tonight, my friend, we party with Rex and his family."

Chapter 5 - A Little Night Work

April nights were chilly in the 'Burbs. By nightfall, most good and godfearing people were indoors. Everyone knew that danger lurked in the night, from giant serpents, deranged sorcerers and D-Bees, to Cyber-Snatchers, street gangs, criminals and Coalition soldiers on patrol. It was best to stay inside, and if that wasn't possible, you didn't want to draw attention to yourself. That didn't stop plenty of people from going out at night, but most were scoundrels, out-of-towners, the desperate or the dangerous. Viper and Goliath fell into the last category.

Rex had put the boys to bed after telling them a bedtime story. It was inspired by one of the jobs he had a few months back, out east in Dinosaur Swamp. Rex and his fellow Juicers had run into Splugorth Slavers. Rex embellished the story a bit about a damsel in distress, hungry dinosaurs and a Cyber-Knight coming to her rescue. The boys hung on every word until finally they couldn't keep their eyes open anymore and had drifted off to sleep. Rex kissed them both on the forehead and as he had done many times before, he swore a quiet oath to them:

"My sons, the world is a crazy place. Both of you and your mother are the only things that make any sense to me. The choices I've made, I know in my heart are the right ones for us. The man that is your father will return to you, I promise."

Rex felt a lump in his throat and felt as if he was on the verge of tears. He could hear his wife coming up behind him and she embraced him.

"Why do you say that to them all the time, Rex?" asked Rachel, looking up into his eyes, seeing that something was different this time.

"I need to remind myself who I am," he said and returned her embrace. "The power coursing through my body, the feelings of being superior, stronger, faster. I can't escape them. Sometimes I feel lost and not the man I once was. If only you knew, just for a second, how I see the world, the crystal clarity of it all and how sometimes the world seems to stand still while I move through it like an observer."

Rex paused to take a breath and just hold on to his wife.

"I can't help but think that once I go through the detox process I'll be a shell of the man I once was. That . . . I'll be nothing."

Rachel's body stiffened and her face took on that stern look when she disciplined the boys.

"You're their father! You're my husband. Is that nothing?"

some reason he wouldn't talk anymore, instead he uses sign language and sometimes Telepathy. And while he was always one of the sweetest men Rachel had ever known, sometimes a rage would overcome Bruce that would turn him into a caged animal. Fortunately the rages were infrequent, and only when his alter ego, *Shadow*, was in a fight. Seeing Rex, Rachel and Jason walking over, Uncle Bruce collected all the balls and started to juggle them. The boys began to complain that he was teasing them again when he tossed one of the balls towards Rex. The Juicer caught it with his free hand and smiled. Todd turned around to chase after the ball and was delighted to see his Dad walking towards him holding Jason in his arms and Mom walking at his side. Seeing his parents, Todd ran over towards his Dad, embracing him in a big hug.

"Are you going to stay for my game, too?" he asked, looking up at his Dad.

"I'll be with you guys all day. And tonight after dinner, maybe we can kick the ball around a little," Rex replied, happy to be with his family at last.

Today was going to be better than he thought, Rex decided as he and his family walked back to the soccer field, where halftime would be ending and Jason would be finishing his big game.

* * *

Viper and his fellow Juicer had spent the better part of a day trying to track down Rex. How could you miss the guy, he thought, it's not like there were that many Juicers in town, especially with a blond Mohawk. He had finally resorted to using one of his City Rat contacts called Stags.

Stags was a D-Bee kid, and from appearances looked like a large, humanoid rat man. He was tall and lanky, had a long, pointed, pink rat nose with hairs sticking out like a mustache. He had matted tan fur and smelled like he lived in the sewers. The City Rat was wearing torn and faded jeans, and a leather vest for a jacket. He also wore some kind of bag around his neck, which he claimed was his good luck piece. Viper had seen the contents once, which consisted of bones from a small rodent, two glass marbles, a piece of copper and a wad of string. The D-Bee was now leading Viper and his partner Goliath through a series of burnt out buildings towards the center where there was an open field. From a distance, Viper could see a man a head above the rest cheering and waving. The hair was neater than usual, but it appeared to be Rex.

"Damn," Viper muttered out loud.

"Sees, I tolds yous he wass heres ands hes lefts the Cyber-Docs likes a news mans," responded the D-Bee, opening his palm towards the Juicer. "Nows yous pays Stags as promiseds."

Viper couldn't stand the way the D-Bee spoke. Everything he said practically ended in an "S." The anger in Viper was swelling and he would have loved nothing more than to disembowel the rat man. In fact, his hands had moved toward his Vibro-Blades when he noticed something. Rex wasn't alone. He and some cute chick were talking to one of the rug rats that Viper could see running all over the place. Could Rex be a family man? thought Viper. No, it couldn't be that easy.

"Good job, Stags. You did so well, in fact, that I'm gonna give you a bonus." The rat man's nose twitched and his mouth opened to reveal a toothy grin as he put his hand out again. However, before any money was placed in the D-Bee's outstretched hand, Viper